WHISPERS OF SHIVA

A Journey of Faith Through Everyday Signs and Dreams

RAAJAN

INDIA • SINGAPORE • MALAYSIA

Copyright © Rajan Sharma 2025
All Rights Reserved.

ISBN
Paperback 979-8-89777-916-1
Hardcase 979-8-89906-279-7

This book has been published with all efforts taken to make the material error-free after the consent of the author. However, the author and the publisher do not assume and hereby disclaim any liability to any party for any loss, damage, or disruption caused by errors or omissions, whether such errors or omissions result from negligence, accident, or any other cause.

While every effort has been made to avoid any mistake or omission, this publication is being sold on the condition and understanding that neither the author nor the publishers or printers would be liable in any manner to any person by reason of any mistake or omission in this publication or for any action taken or omitted to be taken or advice rendered or accepted on the basis of this work. For any defect in printing or binding the publishers will be liable only to replace the defective copy by another copy of this work then available.

Dedicated to all Shiv followers

This book is a heartfelt offering to all seekers of truth, wisdom, and divine grace. It is for the Shiv *Bhakts*, whose unwavering faith illuminates the path for others, and for those who are navigating life's uncertainties, searching for meaning, purpose, and solace.

If you have ever found yourself lost in the chaos of life, struggling with unanswered questions, or longing for inner peace, know that Shiva's presence is always near. Whether you face challenges in relationships, career, or within your own mind, this book serves as a reminder that no struggle goes unseen, and no soul is ever truly alone.

To the weary hearts, the seekers of hope, and those standing at the crossroads of life—this book is for you. Shiva does not merely exist in temples and scriptures; *He* lives within us, speaking through signs, dreams, experiences, and the whispers of our soul. *His* guidance is subtle yet profound, always leading us towards the path we are meant to walk.

Regardless of where you are on your spiritual journey—whether you are a devoted follower or someone just beginning to explore Shiva's presence—this book invites you to embrace *His* wisdom, surrender to *His* grace, and trust in *His* divine plan. It is a testament to the unbreakable bond between the seeker and the divine, a reminder that even in our darkest moments, Shiva's light never fades.

As you turn these pages, may you find strength in surrender, clarity in uncertainty, and peace in faith. May Shiva's boundless love guide you through every challenge, leading you to a life of purpose, fulfilment, and spiritual awakening.

With deepest gratitude and blessings, may this book serve as a guiding light on your journey.

Contents

Pretext: What's in the book

Deep inside, we all seek comfort, guidance, and a connection beyond this temporary world. **Aaraj's** story is no different. For him, that connection has always been with Bhagwan Shiva—the ever-present, kind, and powerful force in life. Shiva's presence is not just a matter of faith—it is an undeniable truth that has shaped Aaraj's journey, whispering answers through dreams, signs, and life's unexpected turns.

So why am I writing this book?

Because Shiva's divine orchestrations are too profound to be kept within me alone, my experiences are not just personal—they are universal, reflecting the hidden hand of destiny that touches every seeker. Through this book and Aaraj's story, I hope to reveal how Shiva communicates with us, guides our paths, and how *His* wisdom can illuminate even the darkest corners of our existence.

Shiva's presence is subtle yet undeniable. *He* speaks to us through coincidences, gut feelings, and moments of silent reflection. *His* guidance is felt in the joys and struggles of life, in the unexpected blessings and painful trials that shape our souls. The path *He* lays out is not always easy. Every lesson, hardship, and moment of grace is part of *His* divine plan, leading us closer to our true purpose.

At the heart of this journey lies the profound truth of karma—the universal law that governs our actions and their consequences. Shiva, the ultimate destroyer of ignorance and granter of wisdom, ensures that we reap what we sow. When we align ourselves with dharma (righteousness), we harmonise with *His* cosmic will. But when we stray, we find ourselves caught in the cycle of suffering, forced to confront the weight of our actions.

Yet, Shiva is not just a disciplinarian; *He* is a loving guide, a compassionate protector, and an ever-present force of transformation. Even in our lowest moments, when doubt clouds our faith, *He* stands beside us, offering strength, clarity, and the courage to move forward. *He* does not promise a life free of pain, but *He* does promise that no pain is without purpose, and no seeker is ever truly alone.

Through Aaraj's journey, I have realised that true fulfilment does not come from material success or societal validation, but from Shiva's deep companionship and guidance. *His* presence fills the soul with a sense of security, confidence, and most importantly, surrender.

However, walking the path of divine faith is not without challenges. Shiva's ways are mysterious and beyond human comprehension. *He* tests our patience, our perseverance, and our devotion. But for those who remain steadfast, *He* reveals truths that transcend the material world, leading us towards ultimate liberation.

As I share Aaraj's personal encounters with Bhagwan Shiva, I do so with profound gratitude for the lessons, the signs, and the unwavering presence that has guided me through every stage of life. This book is not just a narrative—it is an invitation. An invitation to open your heart, recognise the divine signs in your own life, and embrace Shiva's profound wisdom. For Aaraj, it was Shiva. It could be Jesus, Krishna, Guru Nanak, or any divine presence that guides you.

May these words serve as a beacon for those searching for answers, offering solace, strength, and the unwavering belief that divine's grace is ever-present, ever-guiding, and ever-loving.

In loving memory of my late father,

Man Mohan Sharma,
whose unwavering spirit and
resilience instilled in me the
fire to keep moving forward,
never succumbing to failures.
His wisdom continues to
guide me, lighting my path
even in his absence.

To my mother, **Vimal Sharma**, whose boundless love
and nurturing presence shaped me into the person
I am today. Her unwavering support has been my
greatest strength.

To my dearest brother, my pet **Joey** (late Golden
Labrador), whose love I still miss the most.

To my wife, daughter, sisters, colleagues, and
friends—your love and presence helped me walk
this spiritual path. Even without knowing, you each
played a part in guiding me here. Thank you from the
bottom of my heart.

And to my Guru, my best friend, my greatest, my
God, my inspiration—**Bhagwan Shiva**—whose divine
guidance is the very essence of this book. Without *His*
love, I would have achieved nothing in my life.

Thank you!

Chapter 1

How It Began: The Life-Changing Start of a Spiritual Journey

Childhood is often a delicate balance between innocence and expectation. Aaraj's was shaped by academic pressure, societal norms, and an unspoken longing for love and acceptance. In the fifth grade, life felt overwhelming—a whirlwind of demands with little space for self-reflection or emotional release.

At that young age, Aaraj believed love had to be earned through achievements. But something inside him shattered when his father doubted his ability to clear his exams.

"Why don't my parents love me? Why does Papa think I will fail? What did I do wrong? No one loves me... I want to die."

The weight of these thoughts was unbearable. Frustration boiled over, and in a moment of helplessness, Aaraj banged his head against the wall and kept banging. The sharp sting distracted him from the chaos inside, offering a fleeting sense of control. He kept banging his head.

Then, suddenly—darkness.

A terrifying stillness took over. His vision blurred, and it felt like he was slipping into nothingness for a moment.

Was this the end? Would anyone even care?

He rushed down immediately to his parents' floor. He was just a kid (9 years old), had no idea what was happening, and got scared as a sudden hit on the head blurred his vision for a moment.

He found himself in his parents' arms. The very same parents he believed didn't love him were now holding him with a tenderness he had never felt before.

It wasn't just concern – it was something deeper. A love that expected nothing, a love that had been there all along but had gone unnoticed in the noise of expectations.

In that vulnerable moment, Aaraj realised something profound—Shiva's love doesn't always arrive through mystical visions or grand miracles. Sometimes, it comes through the people around us, their touch, their words, their presence.

His parents, in their simple act of holding him close, became the messengers of the divine.

That moment planted a seed within him—a longing to understand this love that seemed beyond the physical. As Aaraj searched for meaning, he felt a deep, unexplainable pull towards Bhagwan Shiva—the one he called out to in his moment of despair (when he banged his head against the wall).

Shiva's image captivated him—the serene yet powerful presence, the serpents coiled around his neck, the crescent moon on his forehead, the ash smeared across his body. There was something deeply familiar in Shiva; it was as if Shiva had been waiting for Aaraj to notice *Him* all along. And finally, Aaraj, at 9, was in complete awe of Bhagwan Shiva.

Aaraj found solace in *His* teachings.

→ The third eye symbolised an inner vision—an invitation to see beyond surface realities and into the truth of existence.

→ The crescent moon reminded him of life's ever-changing cycles—joy, sorrow, creation, and destruction, all flowing in perfect rhythm.

→ And in Shiva's cosmic dance, Aaraj saw his transformation—the destruction of old beliefs, the birth of a deeper understanding.

Aaraj realised that love was never about validation from others. It was a journey inward, a discovery of the divine spark that had always been within him.

Aaraj's spiritual journey didn't begin by accident. The pain that once pushed him to the edge was a doorway to something greater.

Shiva doesn't always reveal *Himself* in thunderous revelations. More often, *He* works in quiet, unseen ways—through the kindness of a loved one, an unexpected moment of peace, or even a deep inner knowing that whispers,

"You are not alone."

When Aaraj felt unloved that night, Shiva sent his parents to hold him.

→ When Aaraj searched for meaning, Shiva led him to *His* wisdom.

→ And in every moment since, *He* has continued to guide him, not with loud answers, but with subtle signs that appear exactly when Aaraj needs them most.

You don't have to search for *Him* in distant places. *He* is in the warmth of a loved one's embrace, the stillness that follows a storm, and the quiet reassurances that arrive when you least expect them.

When we are lost in despair, it is easy to overlook *His* presence. But if we pause for a moment, we will see that Shiva is always there, gently guiding us back to the light.

And that is the greatest love of all.

Key Takeaway: *Spiritual awakening often begins in moments of deep questioning and uncertainty. Surrendering to the divine and embracing faith can open doors to transformation, clarity, and a higher purpose in life.*

Chapter 2

A Miracle, A Message, A Lifelong Devotion

Some moments in life change us forever. They don't arrive with grand announcements but leave behind a mark – a shift in how we see the world.

For Aaraj, one such moment came through, an event that captured the hearts and minds of an entire nation. News spread like wildfire in the 1990s: Bhagwan Shiva was drinking milk.

It began as a media sensation, with people rushing to temples, eager to witness what many called a miracle. Was it a divine phenomenon? Was it a coincidence? Or was it, as sceptics claimed, mere science at play?

At the time, none of these questions mattered to him. All Aaraj knew was that he felt an unshakeable pull toward Shiva – a call to be part of something greater than himself.

That day, Aaraj stood before the idol of Shiva in his home temple, his hands trembling as he held a bowl of milk. He wasn't there for a spectacle or proof; he was there with faith.

As Aaraj offered the milk, something extraordinary happened. Before his eyes, the milk disappeared, accepted by the divine.

Aaraj froze. His heart pounded. He had seen videos of this happening on TV, but it felt different here, in the sacred quiet of his home. It wasn't just a miracle for the world but a message meant for him.

Overcome with emotion, Aaraj rushed to tell his parents. "Come see it for yourself!" he urged them. Yet, nothing happened when they tried to offer the milk. Shiva had chosen to reveal this only to Aaraj.

For a brief moment, Aaraj felt disappointed. But as he sat in quiet reflection, a realisation dawned: some experiences are meant to be deeply personal, and some messages are meant only for those ready to receive them.

This was *His* sign. Aaraj's moment of connection.

That single moment became a turning point in his life. Aaraj made a silent vow to Shiva: to begin each day with *His* name on his lips before any food touched his body.

What started as a simple act became his foundation. The morning bath, the chants, the puja weren't just rituals anymore; they were Aaraj's daily conversations with the divine.

Years passed. Life, as it does, brought its share of joys and struggles. But through every high and low, Shiva remained his constant.

Aaraj looks back and realises: the true miracle was never about the milk. The miracle was in the devotion it ignited, the unwavering faith that has guided him ever since.

That day, Shiva drank the milk to show him *He* was there. But over time, Aaraj has learned that Shiva's messages don't always come in grand miracles.

Sometimes, they appear in a moment of stillness, in an inner whisper, in a dream, in an unexpected answer when we need it most.

Key Takeaway: The signs are there. Shiva is always speaking. The question is: Are we listening? Divine interventions often come in unexpected ways, reaffirming our faith and guiding us towards lifelong devotion. When we remain open to receiving signs, we recognise that every miracle carries a deeper message meant to shape our spiritual path.

Chapter 3

The Turning Point

Struggles, resilience, and unexpected encounters with the divine shape life's journey. Aaraj's path has been no different. As he transitioned from the structured world of academics to the unpredictable realities of adulthood, Aaraj grappled with responsibilities, self-doubt, and the deeper questions of existence.

At just 21, the weight of adulthood pressed heavily upon him. Survival demanded relentless effort, and every day was a test of endurance. Aaraj juggled multiple jobs—working as a compounder in a homoeopathic clinic for just ₹800 a month, delivering electricity bills for ₹10 each, and serving as a principal, teacher, and caretaker at a small village school for ₹600 a month. Each role brought its challenges, yet beneath the hardship, a quiet force guided him, whispering that every struggle carried a purpose far greater than Aaraj could yet comprehend.

Amidst these trials, Aaraj found solace in Shiva.

As his professional journey progressed, Aaraj found himself in the advertising industry, toiling for three and a half years in a fast-paced, high-pressure environment. But even as he climbed the ladder of career success, inner turmoil never left his side.

One particularly difficult day, overwhelmed by professional struggles, Aaraj reached his breaking point. Frustration clouded his mind.

"How can he (the boss) say that I can't do it? I didn't expect this from him. If he doesn't believe in me, why keep me? I just want to leave this place—sooner rather than later."

He thought of escaping the relentless demands of the material world. A tempting illusion of relief.

But something deep within him refused to surrender. An unseen but deeply felt force urged him to seek comfort in the one place that had always brought him peace—Shiva Temple in Chhatarpur, Delhi.

It was a Monday, a day devoted to Bhagwan Shiva. Aaraj walked into the temple carrying a storm within him, hoping to find calm in *His* presence.

As the evening Puja Aarti filled the air with sacred chants, Aaraj stood in the crowd, yet felt utterly alone. Tears streamed down his face as Aaraj surrendered his burdens to the divine, seeking answers that Aaraj hadn't been able to find elsewhere.

That's when it happened.

As Aaraj left the temple, lost in thought, he noticed a beggar—a frail figure standing alone, his presence striking in its simplicity.

Moved by instinct, Aaraj reached into his pocket to offer him money. But to his surprise, he gently refused. Instead, he pointed at the prasad in Aaraj's hand, seeking only a portion of the sacred offering.

The beggar's humility stirred something within him. Aaraj handed him the prasad and turned to leave, but an unexplainable force made him hesitate. A voice within insisted,

"Turn back. Offer him help."

Aaraj turned.

The beggar had gone.

The open ground where he had stood was empty—no sign of movement, no place he could have disappeared into. One moment he was there, the next, he had vanished.

A chill ran through Aaraj. This was no ordinary encounter.

Had Shiva himself revealed *His* presence in that fleeting moment?

The beggar's sudden disappearance felt like an unspoken message—a reminder that the material world is temporary, that wealth and possessions mean little, and that true fulfilment lies in love, compassion, and devotion.

The Conversation That Continued

Still lost in thought, Aaraj returned home, deeply moved by what had happened. As he settled in, his gaze fell upon the television screen—a yoga programme was playing, featuring a revered yogi (Baba Ramdev) speaking about the very thoughts consuming his mind.

The Yogi Baba spoke of detachment from material concerns, the emptiness of seeking external validation, and the importance of surrendering to a higher purpose.

It felt as though the divine conversation Aaraj had begun at the temple was now continuing – this time, through the screen before him.

Moments later, Aaraj shared his experience with his parents. To his astonishment, they too had been watching the same programme in another room, reflecting on the same truths that had stirred his soul.

Coincidence? No. It was Shiva's way of reinforcing *His* message.

That day, everything changed.

→ Aaraj understood that struggles are fleeting—mere ripples in the vast ocean of existence.

→ Aaraj learned that Shiva speaks in mysterious ways—through strangers, through silence, through the smallest moments of clarity.

Looking back, Aaraj sees that day as a turning point – when the veil between the material and the spiritual was lifted, revealing the deeper truth beneath.

Since then, Aaraj has walked this path with renewed faith, knowing that no matter how difficult life seems, Shiva is always there—watching, guiding, and reassuring.

The divine plan is real. We just have to listen.

Key Takeaway: Divine guidance is always present – we must be open to seeing it. Life presents crucial moments that redefine our path. Trusting divine guidance during these transitions ensures that we move forward with faith, strength, and a renewed sense of purpose.

Chapter 4

From Self-Doubt to Divine Awakening

From a young age, Aaraj's father set high expectations for him—expectations he struggled to meet. Perhaps Aaraj wasn't showing the promise his father had hoped for, so the seeds of doubt were sown early in his mind. His father's words, spoken time and again, became an unshakeable refrain:

"You will never achieve anything significant in life if you keep wasting time."

That belief, etched into his consciousness, cast a long shadow over his aspirations. Aaraj grew up navigating life with a quiet but persistent fear—

Was he truly incapable? Was he destined for mediocrity?

Academically, Aaraj was average at best. Yet, Aaraj refused to let his circumstances dictate his future. While completing his education through distance learning, Aaraj took on financial responsibilities to support his family. The road ahead was daunting, filled with obstacles that seemed insurmountable.

Rejections in job interviews only reinforced the self-doubt instilled in him. Each failure felt like a painful confirmation of his father's words. The belief that Aaraj was not enough threatened to break his spirit entirely.

And yet, in the depths of his despair, a force greater than himself refused to let him give up—Bhagwan Shiva.

At his lowest, Aaraj turned to Shiva—not just in prayer but in surrender. He sought *His* wisdom, *His* presence, *His* reassurance. If the world saw him as incapable, could Shiva show him another way?

Through devotion, meditation, and deep introspection, Aaraj slowly began to see that his limitations were not real. They were nothing more than illusions—fears woven by years of conditioning.

Shiva was always there, whispering lessons in ways Aaraj never expected.

→ Every failure, *He* reminded Aaraj, was not an end, but a redirection.

→ Every rejection *He* showed Aaraj was clearing the path for something better.

→ Every struggle, *He* assured Aaraj, shaped him into the person Aaraj was meant to become.

Shiva did not remove his hardships—*He* strengthened him through them. *He* became Aaraj's silent mentor, nudging him towards resilience, perseverance, and self-belief.

The timid, insecure boy, Aaraj, once began to transform.

Aaraj started embracing challenges instead of fearing them. With every step forward, he defied the expectations that had once defined him.

Where Aaraj had once questioned his worth, he now felt an unshakeable faith—not just in Shiva but in himself.

Looking back, Aaraj sees his journey not as a story of struggle but transformation.

→ He no longer measures himself by the doubts of others.

→ He no longer fears failure—it is simply a lesson in disguise.

→ He no longer seeks validation – his path is his to walk, and Shiva walks beside him.

The weight of his father's words once threatened to break him. But today, Aaraj realises—those words were never his to carry.

To anyone struggling under the weight of doubt, rejection, or fear, know this:

Your past does not define your future.
You are not bound by the expectations of others.
Your worth is not dictated by society, family, or failures.

Shiva's guidance comes in ways we don't always recognise. But if you open your heart and listen closely, you will see that *He* is always leading you forward.

No challenge is insurmountable. No dream is too distant. All it takes is faith, perseverance, and the courage to believe in the path unfolding before you.

Because in the end, it is not our circumstances that define us—it is how we rise above them that shapes our destiny.

Key Takeaway: *Self-doubt clouds our potential, but surrendering to the divine brings clarity and purpose. When we trust Shiva's guidance, we awaken to our true strength and embrace our path with confidence and faith.*

Chapter 5

A Whisper from Shiva in the Darkest Hour

Life's journey is often unpredictable, marked by moments of solitude that echo louder than words. At 23, while working at an advertising agency, Aaraj found himself weighed down by profound loneliness—an aching void that no conversation or presence seemed to fill. The world around him felt indifferent, and the warmth of understanding seemed distant, almost unreachable.

Amidst this emotional storm, something extraordinary happened—a moment that blurred the line between human connection and divine intervention. It was as if the universe conspired to remind him that we are never truly alone, even in our darkest hours.

One evening, as Aaraj rode his Bajaj scooter back home, his thoughts spiralled into despair. (*Crying…*)

"I have no one to share everything with. Why does everyone have close companions except me? What have I done wrong?"

The questions churned within him, growing heavier with each mile. Tears blurred his vision as Aaraj navigated the empty roads, whispering his pain to Shiva, seeking answers in the silence while continuing to ride his scooter.

Then, out of nowhere, a hand waved in the darkness at the bus stop.

A Stranger, A Sign

It was common in those days to offer lifts to fellow commuters, so Aaraj instinctively stopped. A young woman, seemingly in her twenties, approached and asked if Aaraj was heading in a certain direction. Though his route was different, he offered to take her as far as possible.

As she settled beside him, something shifted. The ride began as another lonely commute; transformed into an unexpected exchange of words, warmth, and understanding.

Sensing Aaraj's distress, she initiated a conversation, not with small talk, but with genuine curiosity. Her words cut through the fog of despair that had enveloped him. She asked questions that no stranger would normally ask, which made him pause, reflect, and, for the first time in a long while, feel heard.

Aaraj found himself opening up, his emotions spilling out without hesitation. She listened—not out of obligation, but with a quiet empathy that felt like a balm to his wounded spirit. As they rode through the dimly lit streets, the loneliness that had suffocated him just moments ago began to fade.

Aaraj lost track of time and his destination and lost himself in the profound simplicity of human connection.

Finally, as they neared her stop, she asked him to pull over. What happened next was beyond anything Aaraj could have imagined.

She turned to him, looked into his weary eyes, and softly requested,

"Take off your helmet."

Perplexed, Aaraj did as she asked. And then, in a gesture as fleeting as profound, she leaned in and kissed him on the cheek.

It wasn't romantic. It wasn't flirtatious. It was something deeper – an unspoken message, a moment of grace, a touch of the divine.

Aaraj sat there, stunned, as she stepped away and disappeared into the night.

As Aaraj rode home, his mind replayed the encounter over and over.

Who was she? Why had our paths crossed at that exact moment? Was it by chance, or was it something more?

And then it struck him—Shiva had answered.

Shiva's guidance doesn't always come in grand miracles. Sometimes, it arrives in the smallest, most unexpected gestures – a word, a look, a fleeting moment that shifts something within us forever.

That night, through the kindness of a stranger, Shiva reminded him of something Aaraj had forgotten—that Aaraj was never truly alone. That even in his lowest moments, *He* was listening, watching, orchestrating signs along his path.

The kiss on his cheek was not just a gesture. It was a symbol of grace. A message that love, connection, and understanding find us when we least expect them. It was a reminder that the universe, guided by the hand of the divine, weaves moments of comfort into our lives precisely when we need them most.

Returning home, Aaraj found himself speaking to Shiva again, this time in gratitude rather than despair.

Aaraj asked *Him* about the girl, who she was, and why she appeared when she did. And in the quiet stillness of his heart, Aaraj felt *His* answer:

"Life's gifts unfold in their own time. When the moment is right, what you seek will find you."

You truly receive *His* love when you need it most. Sometimes, *He* rewards you for your good deeds. Other times, *He* lifts you in moments of despair.

His love doesn't always arrive with thunder and lightning. It finds you in a stranger's kindness, in an unexpected moment of connection, in the gentle reassurance that no matter how lost you feel, you are never truly alone.

And that is the quiet, mysterious grace of Shiva.

Key Takeaway: In our most difficult moments, Shiva's guidance comes in subtle yet powerful ways—through signs, dreams, or inner intuition. Trusting in His presence can illuminate even the darkest paths, reminding us that we are never truly alone.

Chapter 6

The Reflection of Actions in the Mirror of Life

In the intricate dance of life, every action sends ripples across the universe, shaping our journey in ways we often fail to recognise. As Aaraj walked his path, he began to notice how his good or bad deeds found their way back to him. Some arrived as gentle nudges, others as sharp, undeniable lessons.

Through these experiences, Aaraj understood that Shiva's presence is woven into the unseen forces of karma, ensuring that no action goes unnoticed. In His infinite wisdom, *He* does not punish nor reward—*He* merely holds up a mirror, allowing us to see ourselves more clearly.

Aaraj's first encounter with divine justice seemed trivial at first. He once left without paying a parking ticket in a crowded market, dismissing it as an insignificant mistake. But karma's precision is relentless.

Not long after, Aaraj was met with an avalanche of unexpected fines elsewhere – as if the universe was balancing the scales, reminding him that even the smallest acts carry weight.

It was a simple yet profound lesson:

No debt remains unpaid.

Shiva ensures that every choice shapes our destiny, teaching us responsibility and balance.

One of his hardest lessons came in the form of a thoughtless joke. In a moment of carelessness, Aaraj body-shamed someone, never considering the pain he might have caused.

At the time, it felt harmless – a fleeting comment. But life, ever watchful, had its way of teaching him.

In an unexpected turn of fate, Aaraj soon found himself battling the very same imperfections he had once mocked. The universe had set a mirror before him, forcing him to face the consequences of his actions. The reflection was humbling, urging him to tread more carefully, with greater empathy.

This was the first time Aaraj truly grasped the weight of his words, the silent wounds they could inflict, and the unseen forces that ensure we reap exactly what we sow.

Even within the bonds of family, karma's lessons were at play.

Once, in an attempt to protect his sister, Aaraj betrayed her trust by revealing her secrets to his parents. He convinced himself that it was for her own good, but the damage was irreversible. The foundation of his sibling relationship cracked, and no amount of justification could undo it.

Years later, the echo of his actions returned to him. Aaraj confided in his sister-in-law, trusting her with his deepest thoughts—only to have his trust shattered in return.

In its quiet justice, the universe made sure Aaraj understood: Trust is fragile. Once broken, its scars linger far longer than the fleeting moment of betrayal.

Perhaps the most personal lesson of all came through his own vanity.

Aaraj once mocked someone for their baldness, oblivious to the silent insecurities they carried. It was just a passing comment, a careless jest.

And yet, as time passed, Aaraj found himself staring at his own reflection, watching strands of hair fall away, bit by bit.

Shiva, in *His* quiet way, reminded him that what we ridicule in others can become our own test. Physical beauty, strength, and youth are all transient, fragile illusions. True identity does not lie in appearance but in the depth of our character.

The lessons of karma followed him even into the workplace. In moments of arrogance, Aaraj judged a colleague harshly, forming opinions without knowing their struggles. Aaraj allowed gossip to shape his perception, never once questioning its truth.

Then, the wheel turned. Before Aaraj knew it, he was the subject of the same judgement, his character questioned, his struggles unseen.

In this moment of deep humiliation, Aaraj understood Shiva's silent gaze—a 24/7, 365-day mirror reflecting the entirety of our deeds, thoughts, and words.

In the grand scheme of existence, nothing is forgotten. Every kindness returns as a blessing, and every cruelty finds its way back.

Through these countless experiences, Aaraj came to see that karma is not about punishment—it is about learning. Shiva, in *His* boundless compassion, does not seek to hurt us, only to awaken us.

→ For every act of kindness, *He* bestows blessings in abundance.

→ For every moment of cruelty, *He* offers us a chance to feel its weight, grow, and evolve.

Through *His* silent justice, Aaraj finally understood:

True strength lies not in judgement, but in offering understanding.

In walking Shiva's path, Aaraj strives:

→ Not to mock, but to uplift.

→ Not to betray, but to honour.

→ Not to judge, but to see with compassion.

What we send into the world—be it love or pain—will always find its way back to us.

Key Takeaway: *Life is a mirror that reflects our actions, intentions, and choices. Every deed—good or bad—eventually comes back to us, reinforcing the importance of living with integrity, awareness, and alignment with dharma.*

Chapter 7

The Wake Up Call: A Lesson Learned Through Adversity

Life has a way of offering stark reminders—moments that shake us, forcing us to confront the weight of our choices. For Aaraj, one such moment unfolded amidst the chaos of traffic, where the echoes of Bhagwan Shiva's wisdom resounded with undeniable clarity.

It was an ordinary day, yet beneath the humdrum of routine, a quiet whisper nudged at his awareness. A subtle feeling urged him to slow down his car, drive patiently, and be mindful. But caught in the urgency of his desires, Aaraj chose to ignore the divine warning.

And then—impact.

A sudden, violent collision shattered the stillness, sending shockwaves through his consciousness. In the blink of an eye, the world spun out of control.

The scene unfolded in a blur – a bike slammed into the side of his car, its riders thrown onto the unforgiving asphalt. The sickening sound of metal against the car reverberated through him.

Stepping out of his vehicle, Aaraj was hit by a wave of guilt and responsibility. The gravity of his heedlessness lay before him, not in his pain, but in the suffering he had caused.

A husband knelt beside his injured wife, his anguish palpable in the air. His fury found its target in him, his words sharp with grief and fear. And Aaraj—Aaraj did not defend himself.

He stood there, absorbing his anger, because he knew:

→ that this was his doing.

→ that no justification could undo the harm.

→ that Shiva had warned him, and he had not listened.

In that painful moment, Aaraj realised that this was not a mere chance. This was Shiva's intervention—not to punish him, but to awaken him.

He had whispered through his intuition.

He had sent signs in the stillness of his thoughts.

Yet, Aaraj had ignored *Him*.

Now, faced with the raw consequences of his choices, Aaraj saw the truth with searing clarity. Shiva does not impose suffering—*He* offers us opportunities to learn, evolve, and realign.

Amidst the chaos, Aaraj did the only thing left to do: He took responsibility, ensured the injured woman received help, and stood firm in the storm of blame, not as a victim but as someone who had finally understood.

In the days that followed, the weight of the accident haunted him. Aaraj replayed the moment over and over, searching for meaning beyond regret.

And then, in the stillness, Aaraj felt Shiva's presence.

Not as judgement.

Not as a condemnation.

But as compassion.

Through this painful experience, *He* had not forsaken him—*He* had guided him. *He* had given him a lesson, not in punishment, but in transformation.

Shiva doesn't just watch from afar. *He* warns.

→ Through quiet whispers.

→ Through sudden moments of doubt.

→ Through the deep knowing within.

Yet, if we choose to ignore *Him*, the consequences are ours to bear.

Not because *He* punishes us, but because *He* allows us to learn.

This moment of reckoning became a turning point. Aaraj could no longer live heedlessly, dismissing the divine nudges that sought to guide him.

From that day forward, Aaraj vowed to listen.

→ To honour the whispers of caution.

→ To slow down, not just on the road, but in life.

→ To walk with awareness, humility, and reverence for the sacred interconnectedness of all things.

Key Takeaway: For Shiva's love is not about shielding us from consequences, but about awakening us through them. And in that awakening, we find our true transformation. Adversity is often Shiva's way of awakening us to deeper truths. Challenges are not punishments but opportunities for growth, guiding us towards self-awareness, resilience, and a renewed perspective on life.

Chapter 8

The Sacred Weight of Promises

Promises made to the divine are not mere words—they are sacred threads, binding us to forces beyond our understanding. Yet, in the rush of life, they are easy to forget. We pray in desperation, we pledge in longing, and when our wishes are granted, our promises fade into comfort and routine.

Aaraj learned this truth through two profound experiences—moments when divine forces reminded him not with gentle whispers but with unrelenting force.

The Oath to Maa Vaishno Devi
It began in the hallowed mountains of Jammu & Kashmir, at the shrine of Maa Vaishno Devi. Standing before the divine mother, Aaraj's heart heavy with longing, he made a solemn vow:

"Grant me this boon, Maa, and I will return to offer my gratitude at your sacred feet."

Time passed, and Maa fulfilled her part of the promise. The blessing Aaraj had sought was granted. But he… he forgot.

Caught in the flow of daily life, the memory of his vow dimmed. Until one night, the divine sent a reminder Aaraj could not ignore.

One night, in the realm of his dreams, a tiger pursued him with relentless intensity. Its piercing eyes burned with silent reproach, a gaze that cut through his soul.

Aaraj woke up with a start, his heart pounding. This was no ordinary dream. He knew, with an unshakeable certainty, that it was the tiger of Maa Vaishno Devi herself, reminding him of his forgotten promise.

The tiger's presence was not mere symbolism – it was a message, a consequence, a reckoning.

Aaraj remembered that he had made a sacred vow but had failed to honour it.

In that moment of clarity, fear gave way to resolve. He knew what he had to do.

With a heart full of humility, he sought Maa's forgiveness. When the same dream came again, he fell to his knees before the tiger, hands clasped in surrender. He acknowledged his neglect, vowed to fulfil his promise, and sought more time.

And then, the tiger dissolved into mist.

The next morning, Aaraj wasted no time. He embarked on his pilgrimage, returning to Maa Vaishno Devi's abode. With every step, the weight on his soul lightened, replaced by a profound sense of peace.

In that moment, he understood:

Divine promises are not about transactions. They are about integrity, commitment, and acknowledging that the divine's blessings come with the responsibility of remembrance.

A Second Warning: Hanuman's Call

But Aaraj's lesson was not yet complete.

In another moment of deep supplication in his past, he had made a vow to Hanuman Ji, the mighty protector and embodiment of unwavering devotion.

Once again, time eroded his memory.

Once again, Aaraj let the promise slip away.

And once again, the divine sent a messenger.

This time, it was a gorilla.

In his dreams, it chased him relentlessly, its presence filled with an urgency Aaraj could not ignore.

But now, he understood.

He did not need to wait for fear to shake him into action. He had been given a second chance to listen, act, and honour his word.

Without delay, Aaraj fulfilled his promise to Hanuman Ji.

And with that, the haunting of gorilla coming in his dreams ceased.

In its place, a deep, abiding peace settled within him – the kind that only comes when one stands in alignment with the divine.

These experiences taught him a truth far deeper than the fulfilment of promises.

The divine does not need our vows—
It is we who need them.

Maa Vaishno Devi and Hanuman Ji did not seek retribution. They sought his awakening.

Through these sacred bonds, Shiva taught him:

- Promises are not about restriction, but about transformation.
- They do not bind us to an obligation but empower us to grow.
- They are not for the divine's benefit, but for our elevation.

Faith is not a mere plea for blessings. It is a sacred contract that requires trust, commitment, and the courage to walk the path we promise to follow.

When you walk this path with true devotion, the world changes.

- You begin to see each challenge not as an obstacle, but as a stepping stone to self-realisation.
- You no longer fear the unknown because Shiva walks beside you.
- You no longer run from your promises because you understand their purpose.

And in that understanding, you find not just peace, but divine grace.

Key Takeaway: *Promises are not just words; they carry karmic weight and spiritual significance. Honouring commitments, especially those made with sincerity, strengthens our integrity and aligns us with divine truth.*

Chapter 9

The Call to Kedarnath

In the vast expanse of devotion, a sacred resonance exists—a divine call that beckons the faithful to embark upon a journey of spiritual awakening and communion with the divine. For Aaraj, this call manifested through Kedarnath Jyotirlinga—an ancient shrine cradled in the majestic embrace of the Himalayas, where the echoes of Bhagwan Shiva reverberate through eternity.

As a staunch devotee of Shiva, Aaraj had never felt the need to embark on pilgrimages. *His* connection with him had always been deeply internal, unbound by physical places. Yet, destiny had other plans. A seed of longing was unknowingly planted within him, stirred by Instagram reels showcasing the unwavering devotion of the pilgrims at Kedarnath. A quiet whisper grew louder within his soul with each passing reel—a call Aaraj could no longer ignore.

This unspoken desire found an unexpected medium—his colleague, Suvrajit, who was preparing for his pilgrimage to Kedarnath. Suvrajit's journey awakened a sense of yearning in Aaraj, a silent wish to be in his place. But rather than take action, Aaraj chose patience, trusting that when the time was right, Shiva himself would summon him.

To bridge the distance between himself and Kedarnath, Aaraj made a humble request to Suvrajit:

A small rock from the sacred land of Kedarnath hills.

When Suvrajit returned, bearing both prasad and the rock, Aaraj felt an indescribable connection—a piece of Kedarnath had now come to reside with him.

For 51 consecutive Mondays, Aaraj performed a sacred ritual, offering Jal (water mixed with Ganga water) to the rock and silently invoking the divine with each prayer. Then, on the cusp of the 52nd Monday, it happened—the call came. Shiva had summoned him.

The Journey Begins

With unwavering faith, Aaraj began his preparations. But every pilgrimage has its tests. His colleagues, eager to accompany him, insisted Aaraj shouldn't travel alone. His wife, too, voiced her concern. Yet, deep within, Aaraj knew—this was meant to be a solitary journey. A path that Aaraj had to walk alone, unburdened by distractions, in the presence of his Kedar Baba.

With a heart brimming with anticipation, Aaraj set out. The journey to Kedarnath was as challenging as it was breathtaking, winding through valleys and towering peaks, each step shedding the weight of worldly concerns. But as Aaraj climbed higher, exhaustion crept in, and doubts began to whisper.

"Baba," he murmured, barely audible in the mountain winds, "this journey is too difficult for me. I fear I may not reach your sacred abode. Help me."

And then, as if in response, he stumbled upon a crystalline stream, its waters glacial and pure, cascading down the slopes with an energy that felt almost divine. Instinctively, Aaraj cupped his hands and drank. A surge of strength coursed through his weary body, as if Shiva had infused him with renewed vigour. Aaraj knew, without a doubt, that he was walking this path with him.

Reaching Kedarnath was not the end of his trials. Aaraj had vowed to stay only within sight of the temple, refusing any accommodation that did not meet this condition. This devotion led to a moment of divine intervention.

As Aaraj stood in line to purchase a VIP ticket for a private puja, an unexpected offer came his way — a stranger ahead of him offered to share his ticket at a fraction of the cost. Aaraj:

Was this merely a coincidence? Or yet another sign of Shiva's hand guiding my steps?

Curious, Aaraj accepted the offer, and as they walked together, Aaraj was drawn to a question that had suddenly taken root in his mind. Turning to a young boy in the group, Aaraj asked:

"What is your Gotra? (a lineage descended from a common male ancestor)"

His answer sent shivers down his spine.

"Vatsa."

The same as his.

Aaraj stood frozen, his heart overwhelmed by the realisation of Shiva's intricate design. Every step, every decision, and meeting was orchestrated by *His* divine will. He was exactly where he was meant to be.

That night, at 2 a.m., Aaraj stood before the sacred Shivling of Kedarnath. The flickering light of lamps cast an ethereal glow, and the air was thick with the chants of fellow devotees. As he placed his offerings, he felt an overwhelming surge of peace, gratitude, and surrender.

Shiva had not only called him to Kedarnath—*He* had walked with him, strengthened him, and revealed *Himself* in the most unexpected ways.

As Aaraj bid farewell to the temple, his heart brimmed with an unshakeable truth: one does not visit Kedarnath by choice. One only goes when Shiva calls.

As Aaraj descended from the sacred peaks, he carried more than just memories. He carried the knowledge that he was never truly in control.

Every step he took, every sign he followed, had been guided by Shiva's unseen hand. Kedarnath was not just a destination but a revelation, a journey of surrender and faith.

In the end, we are all mere travellers, walking paths illuminated by *His* divine will, one step at a time.

Key Takeaway: When the divine calls, it is not just a journey of distance but of transformation. Shiva's summons to sacred places like Kedarnath is an invitation to cleanse the soul, seek deeper truths, and surrender to a higher purpose.

Chapter 10

A Gift For Bhagwan Shiva

On a tranquil afternoon, Aaraj was grateful to Bhagwan Shiva. It was as if *He* had reached into the depths of his heart, plucking out his unspoken desires and weaving them into reality—without a single word spoken. A smile lingered on his lips as Aaraj whispered his thanks, recognising the depth of his understanding and the boundless love he so effortlessly bestowed upon him.

A quiet yearning stirred within him – a longing to give something in return. How could Aaraj bring joy to the heart of the one who had given him everything? With sincerity brimming in his soul, Aaraj closed his eyes and offered a simple prayer:

"Show me the path to bring joy to your divine soul."
"Grant me the privilege to serve you—to be your instrument in extending kindness and aid to those in need."

As evening descended, Aaraj sought solace in a spa, hoping to unwind amidst life's ceaseless tides. The gentle hands of the masseuse worked through the tension in his body, but soon, a casual question changed the course of his night.

"Your tattoo… is that Bhagwan Shiva?" she asked, looking at Aaraj's tattoo on his left arm.

Aaraj smiled, a flicker of recognition dancing between them.

"Yes," Aaraj replied, "*He* is the guiding force of my life."

Her eyes lit up as she reached for her phone, revealing her wallpaper—an image of Shiva himself. "I'm a devotee too," she said softly, her voice carrying the weight of unwavering faith.

As our conversation unfolded, she shared something unexpected—it was her birthday. She had planned to finish work early, but fate had presented her with one final appointment—Aaraj's.

At that moment, realisation struck like a beacon in the night.

This was it—Shiva's answer to his prayer.

The path to bringing joy to his divine soul had unfolded before him, not through grand gestures, but through a simple act of kindness.

Determined to honour the gift of this moment, Aaraj made a decision. He would end his massage at the same moment.

Despite her protests, Aaraj insisted.

"You deserve to celebrate your special day without delay."

Aaraj placed a generous tip in her hands—not just to express appreciation for her service but also as a token of Shiva's boundless grace. He wished her a beautiful year ahead with a warm smile and bade her farewell.

A deep sense of peace washed over him as he stepped out into the cool night air. Shiva had spoken—not through words, but through circumstance, intuition, and the simple joy of giving.

Aaraj understood then that serving Shiva does not always mean grand sacrifices or rituals. It can be as simple as bringing a smile to another soul, extending a hand in kindness, or lightening someone's burden.

Shiva's love is not bound by temples or offerings—it flows through every act of selflessness and every moment of compassion. When we help another, we reflect *His* boundless grace, allowing *His* love to manifest through us.

And in those moments, we do not just worship *Him*. We walk alongside *Him*.

Key Takeaway: *Devotion is not measured by grandeur but by sincerity. A true offering to Shiva is not material but comes from a heart filled with faith, love, and surrender.*

Chapter 11

Faith, Confidence, and the Power of Belief

In life's uncertainties, where doubt and hesitation often cloud our path, faith becomes our guiding light, illuminating the way forward with unwavering certainty. For Aaraj, that beacon of hope has always been Bhagwan Shiva, whose presence fills him with strength and confidence, even in the face of life's greatest challenges.

One such challenge arose while carrying on relationships, where societal expectations and familial pressures often shape our choices. When his parents began urging him to marry, their well-intentioned pleas became a constant reminder of the ticking clock and the weight of expectations placed upon him.

At that time, Aaraj wasn't ready for marriage—not because he feared commitment, but because he knew deep within that the moment wasn't right.

Torn between wanting to please his parents and staying true to himself, he wrestled with conflicting emotions. Yet, in those moments of uncertainty, his faith in Shiva gave him the courage to stand firm, trusting that the right path would unfold in time.

As Aaraj navigated the world of online matrimonial sites to honour his parents' pressure, he encountered one dead end after another. Conversations felt forced, connections were fleeting, and each meeting left him feeling more adrift. Doubt began to creep in.

Then, one evening, in a moment of frustration and clarity, he made a bold declaration to his mother, not out of arrogance, but from a deep-seated belief in his journey and Shiva's guidance.

"I will only marry once I earn more than ₹50,000 a month," Aaraj proclaimed.

At the time, Aaraj was earning ₹15,000—a stark contrast to the goal he had just set. Yet, even as the words left his lips, a quiet sense of calm washed over him. It wasn't an empty statement; it was a promise—to himself and Shiva.

With unwavering conviction, Aaraj took a piece of chalk and scrawled his words on the kitchen wall, turning them into a visible testament to his resolve. That moment marked a turning point—not just in his career, but in his faith. He had trusted Shiva, and he knew Shiva would lead the way.

The path ahead was anything but easy. Setbacks, failures, and disappointments became familiar companions. Yet, through every challenge, Shiva's presence was his anchor. *His* silent whispers reminded him to push forward, to believe in his potential, and to stay resilient in the face of adversity.

There were moments when doubt tried to take root, but every time Aaraj looked at the words on the kitchen wall, he felt a renewed sense of purpose. Shiva had given him the vision—now, it was his turn to act.

Then, as if by divine intervention, the day arrived. Within 3 years of perseverance, his salary crossed a higher threshold than the set target—₹80,000.

Standing at that milestone, Aaraj knew this wasn't just his achievement. It was *His* grace. *His* hand had guided him, *His* presence had fortified him. What once seemed like an impossible dream had become his reality, not through mere hard work alone, but through faith, surrender, and divine timing. Today, as Aaraj stands at the threshold of a new chapter, his heart is full of gratitude. Aaraj no longer fears the unknown because Aaraj has seen Shiva's hand in his journey. Whatever comes next, Aaraj knows one thing with certainty—Aaraj is never alone.

With Shiva by his side, all things are possible.

———

***Key Takeaway:** Unshakeable faith and self-confidence have the power to shape our reality. When we truly believe in Shiva's guidance and trust in our own potential, we unlock the strength to overcome obstacles and manifest our destiny.*

Chapter 12

0.0001%: Finding Love and Confidence Through Faith

In life's journey, love and destiny often seem like forces beyond our control. The search for companionship can be filled with uncertainty, self-doubt, and disappointment. Yet faith has the power to anchor us, giving us the strength to persist even when the path ahead seems unclear. For Aaraj, that faith was in Bhagwan Shiva, whose presence gave him the courage to embrace life's uncertainties and trust in the process.

After reaching his long-awaited career milestone, he stepped into relationships with renewed confidence, hoping to find his life partner. However, despite his best efforts, disappointment met him at every turn. Rejections stung, self-doubt crept in, and he sometimes wondered if he was chasing an illusion. But deep down, he held onto one truth—Shiva had a plan, even if Aaraj couldn't see it yet.

It was in this spirit of trust and surrender that Aaraj met Jane during his office induction. From the very first conversation, something about her captivated him—her warmth, intellect, and effortless charm. They started chatting online regarding work, but didn't know how the chats would progress. One day, encouraged by an inner voice, Aaraj made a bold move and invited her for a beer. Aaraj had no expectations, no fear of rejection— just the simple belief that whatever was meant to be, would be.

To his surprise, she accepted.

As they spent more time together, their bond deepened in ways Aaraj hadn't anticipated. Conversations flowed effortlessly, laughter came naturally, and Aaraj found himself drawn to her in a way he couldn't explain. Yet, beneath this growing connection, he was aware of a challenge—Jane was navigating the complexities of a past relationship, uncertain about what the future held.

One evening, she hesitated, expressing her concerns. She feared that Aaraj's growing feelings might lead to heartbreak, that the uncertainty of her emotions might cause him pain. At that moment, Aaraj had a choice— he could step away, or he could trust in Shiva's divine timing.

With a heart full of faith, he simply asked her for the smallest possibility—0.0001%—to keep hope alive.

That tiny fraction of hope was enough.

What followed was a journey of patience, understanding, and unwavering trust in the path that Shiva was unfolding. With time, love found its way. What had once been a sliver of possibility transformed into a lifelong partnership, bound by faith and divine grace. They got married.

As he looks back, he sees the profound wisdom of Shiva's timing. *His* guidance led him not only to love but also to the confidence to trust in himself. Now, as Aaraj celebrates his life with Jane, he is reminded that faith is not just about believing in what is certain—it is about embracing the unknown with unwavering trust.

Key Takeaway: Faith has the power to transform doubt into confidence and setbacks into stepping stones. When you trust Shiva, you are not just surrendering to fate—you are stepping into a journey where every challenge leads you closer to your destiny. The smallest seed of faith, even 0.0001%, can be enough to change your entire life. Trust in the divine, take bold steps, and let faith guide the way.

Chapter 13

Finding Light in the Darkness

Life weaves together moments of joy and sorrow, forming a complex sequence of existence. Often, in the most ordinary of moments, we are confronted with the deepest truths—truths that shake us, force us to reflect, and sometimes, push us to the edge.

During a casual office outing, Aaraj first glimpsed the depths of human suffering in a way he had never experienced before. As laughter and conversation filled the air, Manni, a colleague, suddenly spoke words that cut through the moment like a dagger.

"Life is not that beautiful," Manni said, his voice laden with anguish. "Every day, I wake up wondering why I am not dead."

Manni's words hung heavily, a haunting reminder of the silent battles we often fail to see. At the time, Aaraj was unsettled but unaware of how soon he would find himself standing at the edge of despair.

Not long after, darkness crept into his life—personal struggles, professional failures, and an overwhelming sense of isolation. The burdens felt unbearable, as if the air around him had thickened, making breathing hard.

Aaraj began questioning everything—even his existence.

In the depths of his suffering, he again turned to Bhagwan Shiva, his last refuge, pleading with *Him* in desperation:

"I have no desire to live. Now I understand why Manni said that that day. I don't want to live in this world. Please kill me. I don't want to get up in the morning."

With tears streaming down his face and his soul crying out for release, Aaraj begged for an end to his torment. Yet, amidst the silence of his anguish, a flicker of Shiva's presence began to emerge—a faint but steady light breaking through the darkness.

One evening, when the weight of his burdens felt unbearable, Aaraj made a desperate plea:

"Give me a sign. Show me that I am not alone."

In that moment, an unexplainable peace washed over him, as if Shiva had whispered into his soul, reminding him that *He* was there, always had been, and always would be. The pain didn't vanish instantly, but something within him shifted—Aaraj knew he was being held, protected, and guided.

Looking back, he realises that his faith in Shiva saved him. It gave him the strength to rise from despair, believe in the purpose behind his struggles, and keep moving forward even when everything felt impossible.

Aaraj knows it's not easy when you feel like you have no one to rely on, when the world seems against you, and instead of comfort, you face mistrust, blame, and isolation. When every effort feels futile, and you begin to wonder:

Why am I even here? Who needs me? Does anyone truly care?

The weight of despair can feel unbearable, and the silent pain can drive even the strongest souls towards self-destruction.

But I promise you this—you are not alone. Shiva listens when no one else does. *He* does not judge, blame, or abandon. *He* simply embraces your pain and strengthens you in ways beyond your understanding.

So, keep asking *Him* questions. Ask *Him* why you are suffering, pour out your pain to *Him*—because *He* will answer. Maybe not immediately or in the way you expect, but *His* guidance will come. And when it does, you will find clarity, comfort, and a renewed sense of purpose.

No matter what happens, trust *Him*. Everything happens for a reason—and in the grand scheme of life, it happens for good. Even your pain shapes you, strengthens you, and leads you towards something greater. Hold on. *He* will never abandon you.

__Key Takeaway:__ Even in our darkest moments, there is always a guiding light. Shiva's presence reminds us that challenges are not the end but a path to transformation, leading us towards strength, wisdom, and renewal.

Chapter 14

Aligning with Shiva's Teachings

As a devotee of Bhagwan Shiva, Aaraj's journey has been a complicated sequence of events woven with moments of clarity and self-reflection, alongside periods of misguided beliefs and temptations. The path to Shiva is not always straightforward—it is filled with challenges that test one's resolve, understanding, and commitment to the truth.

One such challenge stemmed from a common misconception—the belief that indulging in alcohol and smoking weed is somehow aligned with Shiva's preferences. Many people justify these habits by citing Shiva's association with bhang, dhatura, or other substances, using this as an excuse for self-indulgence. However, true devotion is not about imitating rituals without understanding their deeper meaning—it is about embodying the essence of Shiva's teachings.

A profound lesson lies in the Samudra Manthan, the churning of the ocean. When the deadly poison halahal surfaced, threatening to destroy the world, Shiva selflessly consumed it, holding it in his throat rather than swallowing it. This act turned his throat blue, earning him the name Neelkantha—the one who bears suffering for the welfare of all.

This was not an act of indulgence; it was an act of sacrifice. Shiva did not take poison for pleasure – he bore it to protect the universe. This moment reveals Shiva's true nature: a divine force that absorbs negativity without being consumed. To misuse this symbolism as a justification for intoxication is to misunderstand its essence entirely.

For a time, Aaraj too fell into this misconception, believing that drinking alcohol or smoking was, in some way, a tribute to Shiva. But as his spiritual connection deepened, Aaraj began to see the flaws in this reasoning. If his goal was to move closer to Shiva, how could he walk a path that clouded his judgement and dulled his senses?

Quitting alcohol was a turning point in his spiritual journey. Aaraj realised that Shiva's path is one of clarity, self-discipline, and heightened awareness—qualities incompatible with substances that diminish control over one's mind.

However, the journey towards spiritual purity is ongoing. While Aaraj has left alcohol behind, he acknowledges that smoking remains a challenge.

Though he is not an addict, he recognises that it still acts as a barrier to his spiritual growth. And if he truly seeks to embody Shiva's teachings, he must consciously work towards letting go of all that holds him back.

Shiva does not seek ritualistic imitation – he seeks sincere transformation. True devotion is not in mere words or surface-level acts but in a life of integrity, humility, and self-awareness. It demands that we look inward, question our motivations, and make choices that align with compassion, wisdom, and detachment from illusory pleasures.

The path to Shiva is one of elevation, not escapism. As Aaraj continues his journey, he reminds himself that every step towards self-discipline brings him closer to Shiva.

Masturbation

The journey of self-discovery often leads us down unexpected paths, revealing hidden truths and profound revelations. One such turning point came when Aaraj realised that even the most personal experiences could serve as a medium for divine guidance.

It began at 21, a time of innocence, curiosity, and exploration. Like many young men, Aaraj navigated the uncharted waters of self-discovery, unaware of the impact it would have on him. His first encounter with masturbation left him bewildered and frightened—his body reacted in ways Aaraj had never anticipated. His penis swelled to an alarming size, sending waves of fear and uncertainty through him. In desperation, Aaraj turned to Bhagwan Shiva, seeking solace in his divine presence.

That night, as Aaraj prayed, a deep calm washed over him. By morning, his body had returned to normal—a sign, a reassurance that he was not alone in his struggles. From that day onward, masturbation became a coping mechanism—a source of comfort during stress, a means to release tension.

Years passed, and as Aaraj entered his 40s, he began to notice subtle yet troubling changes in his body. His hairline receded, his teeth weakened, his eyesight dimmed, and his memory faltered. These signs of ageing and decline left him feeling vulnerable, despite his best efforts to counteract them through conventional means.

Once again, Aaraj sought Shiva's guidance, yearning for clarity amidst his growing concerns. The answer that surfaced within him was unexpected yet profound—Aaraj needed to abstain from masturbation.

At first, Aaraj resisted. Could something so seemingly natural be holding him back? But Aaraj had learned to trust the wisdom of Shiva. And so, he made a choice—

not out of guilt, but out of a desire to align himself with his guidance.

As the days turned into weeks, Aaraj observed subtle yet powerful transformations:

- → His energy surged, like a dormant fire had been rekindled.
- → His hair showed signs of regrowth, his mind felt sharper, and his vision clearer.
- → A renewed sense of vitality coursed through him, replacing the fatigue and sluggishness that had once weighed him down.

It was as if Shiva's hand was guiding him towards restoration and renewal. By surrendering to his wisdom, Aaraj had unlocked a strength beyond the physical, a resilience that transcended the limitations of mortality.

This experience taught him that Shiva's guidance is not about restriction but liberation. True devotion is not just about prayer or rituals; it is about listening, trusting, and aligning our actions with the divine wisdom that flows through us.

By embracing self-discipline, Aaraj had not lost anything—Aaraj had gained clarity, vitality, and a deeper connection to Shiva. And in that surrender, Aaraj found the greatest gift: a path back to wholeness.

Anger

Moments of self-doubt often cast long shadows over our sense of worth, making us question our purpose and potential. These thoughts echo in the corridors of our consciousness, making us wonder:

Am I doing enough?

Yet, amidst this turmoil of uncertainty, a guiding presence exists—Bhagwan Shiva—who sees beyond our imperfections and never ceases to invest *His* love and energy in us.

Like many seekers, Aaraj often grapples with his own flaws, wondering why Shiva continues to guide him despite his shortcomings.

"Why does Shiva have faith in me when I falter? Why does He not turn away when I struggle with the same weaknesses again and again?"

The answer lies in his boundless compassion and wisdom. Shiva does not see us only as we are, but as we can be—as the divine beings we are meant to become.

One of the greatest lessons Shiva has been guiding him through is his struggle with anger. *He* does not scold or condemn him for it; instead, he gently nudges him toward self-awareness, reminding him that anger serves no true purpose. His wisdom is simple yet profound:

> *Replace anger with a smile, reclaim control over your emotions, and let go.*

But his journey is not without setbacks. Despite his best intentions, Aaraj still finds himself succumbing to frustration, only to regret it later. In these moments of failure, Aaraj feels unworthy of Shiva's presence. Aaraj even asks *Him* to withdraw *His* investment in him, to leave him to his weaknesses and just take his breath away from this world.

Yet, *He* never does.

No matter how often Aaraj falls, Shiva remains steadfast in *His* belief in him. *He* does not abandon him in his struggles; instead, *He* continues to guide, uplift, and refine him. *His* love is not conditional—it is an anchor in the storm, holding him steady even when Aaraj feels lost.

With every stumble, Aaraj learns that Shiva's presence is not about perfection but about progress. He does not seek blind devotion; he seeks growth, transformation, and self-awareness. Shiva patiently works with him on his flaws, not to punish him but to help him rise stronger, wiser, and more compassionate.

The true challenge is not Shiva's willingness to guide us—it is our willingness to listen. Too often, we resist *His* wisdom and remain trapped in our doubts, fears, and impulses. We ignore *His* signs, and we wonder why we feel abandoned when we fall.

The truth is, *He* never leaves us – we stray from *Him*.

If we truly embrace our imperfections, acknowledge where we need to change, and sincerely try to improve, Shiva walks with us in every step. No struggle is too big, no weakness too strong—as long as we trust *Him* and walk *His* path with honesty and faith.

For Shiva does not see imperfection as a flaw—*He* sees it as a canvas upon which the masterpiece of our life is waiting to be painted.

Key Takeaway: Overcoming bad habits requires awareness, discipline, and spiritual alignment. By surrendering to Shiva's guidance and embracing self-control, we can break free from negative patterns and move towards a more purposeful life.

Chapter 15

Selfish Journey of Peace

At the height of personal and professional turmoil, Aaraj drowned in a sea of sadness, struggling to stay afloat amidst relentless negativity and despair. Each day felt like an uphill battle, filled with challenges that made him question the purpose of his suffering. Aaraj longed for a sign—a beacon of hope—to guide him through the darkness.

> *"I hateeeeeeee love. There is no such thing as love. Happiness is everything. I want to be happy. I won't kill myself; you kill me if you can't keep me happy and content. This is not the life I want."*

As Aaraj commuted home that evening, while conversing with Shiva on the way, tears streamed down his face, his heart heavy with frustration. In desperation, he cried out to Bhagwan Shiva, his voice trembling with raw emotion:

"Why am I in this mess? Punish me if I am wrong but show me the path to happiness. Is there no one who accepts me as I am, without asking me to change?"

After a few days, amidst this internal storm, Aaraj found an unexpected source of solace—a colleague at work whose presence felt like divine intervention. Bhoomi, too, was devoted to Shiva, and their shared faith became a quiet refuge in his darkest hours.

Her kindness extended beyond words—she would bring prasad from the Shiva temple and offer it to him, a small but profound gesture that felt like Shiva himself was reaching out, reminding him that Aaraj was not alone.

For a time, this newfound friendship felt like a lifeline, a sign that Shiva had indeed heard his prayers to take Aaraj out from the waves of negativity.

But as their friendship blossomed, it sparked suspicion at his home and deepened the existing cracks. Accusations of disloyalty followed, and Aaraj found himself at a painful crossroads again.

So, to preserve peace at home, he decided to distance himself from his friend, even though it meant losing a source of comfort during his struggles.

Through it all, Bhagwan Shiva remained his unwavering anchor, guiding him through the storms, offering solace when Aaraj felt abandoned, and reminding him that no suffering was in vain.

Looking back, Aaraj realises that Shiva's love is limitless, and his compassion is boundless. *He* does not abandon us in our trials but strengthens us to endure them.

He is the ultimate arbiter of karma, ensuring that we reap the bitter and sweet fruits of our actions. Through every challenge, *He* teaches us the lessons we need to grow.

Though the journey has been painful, Aaraj is grateful for the lessons learned, the growth gained, and Shiva's unwavering presence in his life.

In the end, *He* is always there, guiding, loving, and shaping us into the souls we are meant to become.

Key Takeaway: *Seeking peace is not selfish but essential for inner growth. Detaching from external chaos and prioritising one's well-being can lead to a deeper connection with the divine and a more meaningful life.*

Chapter 16

Testing Shiva's Presence

Life is a complicated set of paths where shadows and light intertwine, leading us through twists of joy and sorrow, understanding and conflict. Amid it all, Aaraj found himself caught in the treacherous waters of marital discord, navigating a journey fraught with misunderstandings, miscommunications, and moments of despair.

Yet, even in his darkest nights, one unwavering presence remained—Bhagwan Shiva. His divine grace was the beacon that guided him through the storm, offering him solace, strength, and silent reassurance when everything else seemed to crumble.

As the weight of marital strife bore down on him, Aaraj turned to prayer—his last refuge, his only sanctuary. Night after night, he poured his heart out to Shiva, hoping that *He* would hear his cries and ease the burden of his suffering.

"Why am I always wrong? When someone else makes a mistake, if I react to it, does that make me wrong? Why does this always happen to me? Are you not seeing this, Shiva? Do you think it's my fault? I cannot live like this. Prove that you are with me."

In his anguish, one light kept him grounded—his daughter. Her innocent presence was the only thing anchoring him to sanity. For her sake, Aaraj endured. But even as he clung to her, the unanswered questions tormented him, echoing through the hollow chambers of his heart.

Desperation pushed him to the edge.

Aaraj needed to know if Shiva was truly with him.

He pleaded for a sign, a reassurance that *He* was listening and had not abandoned him in this storm.

With trembling hands and extreme pain, Aaraj made a sacred yet flawed request:

"Shiva, if you are truly watching over me, give me a sign. Let Jane experience a temporary ailment— loose motions—only to wake up completely fine in the morning."

That night, as if answering Aaraj's call, it happened exactly as Aaraj had spoken. Jane (wife) fell ill in the night with an upset tummy, but by sunrise, she awoke refreshed, as if nothing had ever happened.

At that moment, Aaraj was overwhelmed—not with triumph but shame and understanding.

What Aaraj did was not right.

Faith does not need proof. Shiva's presence is not something to be tested – it is something to be felt, trusted, and surrendered to.

Aaraj did not make that request to harm her, nor was it about doubting her. It was about seeking reassurance in a way that Aaraj could not deny. But he realised then that Shiva's signs come in their own time and their way. They do not always arrive as we demand, but they are always there for those willing to see with an open heart.

In the grand sequence of existence—woven with joy and sorrow, love, and longing—Bhagwan Shiva silently watches, patiently guides, and lovingly corrects. He does not abandon us; we are the ones who waver.

True devotion is believing even when there is no visible sign, knowing *He* is always there, watching, guiding, and protecting.

In that understanding, Aaraj found peace, wisdom, and redemption—a testament to the transformative power of faith and Shiva's boundless love.

***Key Takeaway:** The more we try to control everything, the more we suffer. True power comes from surrendering to divine timing. Shiva's presence is not proven through miracles but through the subtle signs, synchronicities, and inner guidance we receive. Faith deepens when we surrender our doubts and recognise His hand in life's smallest moments.*

Chapter 17

Finding Friends

Friendship is a delicate thing, connecting people through shared experiences. Aaraj had no friends and used to be very lonely. In school, Aaraj felt like he didn't belong. Everyone else seemed to have friends, but he was always alone. Aaraj wanted to have friends and wondered if he ever would.

"Everyone has friends, but I don't. Why can't I have some? I also need someone to share my thoughts, fears, and things I can't tell anyone else. I need friends, Shiva."

As he normally does in his most vulnerable moments, Aaraj turned to Shiva again, whispering his silent wishes, hoping *He* would hear his cries. Aaraj prayed for companions, not just friends in passing, but those who would stand by his side through every trial and triumph.

One afternoon, after returning from a cricket match—where the camaraderie of teammates only deepened his loneliness—Aaraj found himself overcome with emotion. As tears soaked his pillow, he pleaded with Shiva for four steadfast friends, those who would walk beside him, even unto death.

Aaraj had no idea that Shiva was already weaving the threads of fate.

And then, as if in divine response, they arrived—Vivek, Neeraj, Aashu, and Sam, in intervals. Each one entered his life in unexpected ways, forever changing its course.

→ Vivek, the irrepressible spirit of mischief, brought laughter in the darkest times.

→ Neeraj, the quiet yet unwavering strength, a friend who stood solid like a rock.

→ Aashu, the brilliance of intellect, whose wisdom and clarity enriched our journey.

→ Sam, the infectious brightness of youth, carried joy like a flame in his heart.

Together, they forged a bond that transcended mere friendship – they became brothers in spirit, tied together by something beyond words, beyond time.

As the years unfolded, this circle grew, welcoming Mayank, Ashish, Akshit, Satya, Avinash, Suvrajit, Vedu, Rajkamal and more—each one a thread in the web of connection and camaraderie, each name etched into the story of his life as a reminder of Shiva's grace.

Even amid laughter and shared experiences, Aaraj remained ever aware of Shiva's guiding presence. *He* was there—not just in his prayers but also in the kindness of his friends, the joy of their bond, and the unseen force that had drawn them together.

Then, in January 2024, an opportunity arose—one that would transform their bond into something even deeper. Aaraj's closest companions, Mayank, Vivek, and Neeraj, embarked on a spiritual pilgrimage together, visiting three sacred Jyotirlingas—Tryambakeshwar, Girisheshwar, and Bhimashankar—along with Shani Shignapur, Shri Mahalakshmi temple, and Shri Siddhivinayak temple in Maharashtra.

This was no ordinary trip; it was a pilgrimage of the soul.

Draped in religious attire, hearts brimming with devotion, they chanted mantras, offered prayers, and surrendered themselves to the divine energy surrounding them. Some say such journeys are meant for the twilight years of life, but they knew the truth—spiritual awakening has no age, and the call of faith knows no time.

In the end, this journey was not just about visiting sacred places. It was a testament to the divine connections that had shaped Aaraj's life, from loneliness to companionship, from longing to fulfilment. For in the embrace of friendship and faith, Aaraj found solace, strength, and the boundless love of Shiva. *His* blessings had been with him every step, turning his silent prayers into living, breathing answers and yet another proof of it.

And so, Aaraj walks forward—never alone, always surrounded by the grace of Shiva and the friends *He* gifted him.

***Key Takeaway:** True friendships are about companionship and shared energy, values, and growth. The right friends uplift, support, and align with your journey, while the wrong ones drain and mislead. Shiva guides us to those who truly belong in our lives.*

Chapter 18

A Divine Gift on Birthday

There are moments when fate weaves together an intricate masterpiece—one so profound that it leaves us in awe of the unseen hand guiding our lives. For Aaraj, such a moment unfolded on his birthday, a day that had once been marked by solitude (he never liked the sudden attention of people) but was now transformed into a celebration of divine intervention and boundless love.

November 25th had always been a day of quiet reflection for him – a time when Aaraj retreated into his own thoughts, embracing solitude. But this year (2016) was destined to be different. This year, his wife, Jane, and he would embark on a journey that would forever change their lives.

For years, they had walked the path of marriage with love, patience, and unwavering commitment, navigating its joys and challenges together. But amidst their happiness and futile disagreements, there remained a silent longing—the dream of parenthood, the hope of hearing the soft laughter of a child filling their home.

In the quiet moments of their journey, Aaraj made a sacred vow—to wait until Jane felt truly ready to embrace motherhood. It was not a decision made under pressure but with love, trust, and deep understanding. And so, Aaraj waited.

Four years passed after their marriage, testing their patience. But they held firm, believing the right time would come, guided by divine will.

And then, like the first light of dawn after a long night, Jane finally felt ready. The dream they had cherished for so long was about to take flight. The anticipation of welcoming their child filled their hearts, made even more special by a beautiful coincidence—their baby was due in November, the month of Aaraj's birth.

Aaraj reveled in the thought of sharing his birthday month with their child, imagining the years ahead, the celebrations, the memories they both would create together. But as his birthday approached, their excitement turned to uncertainty.

Days passed, but the signs of labour did not come. Hope turned into anxiety, and with each moment, the weight of anticipation grew heavier. Jane and Aaraj clung to each other, their hearts whispering unspoken fears.

As he does best in his moments of doubt, Aaraj turned to Bhagwan Shiva—the eternal guardian, the silent observer of all things. With a heart full of longing, he prayed:

"Are you listening? Have you not seen the journey we have walked? You have always been with me—will you not show me a sign now? What's going on? What is your plan?"

And then, on the morning of November 25th—his birthday—Shiva answered.

As Aaraj stood by Jane's side in the delivery room, time seemed to pause. Sanya, their daughter, entered the world—her first cries marking the beginning of a new chapter in their lives.

As Aaraj held her tiny form in his arms at that moment, a realisation washed over him—this was no coincidence. This was Shiva's gift, a divine blessing beyond anything Aaraj could have imagined.

Shiva had granted Aaraj's prayers and given him more than he ever dared to ask for. Shiva had written their daughter's arrival into the very fabric of *His* existence, entwining their fates forever.

In that sacred moment, Aaraj understood:

➜ *He* listens, even when we don't realise it.

→ *He* grants what we seek and the blessings we never thought to ask for.

The birth of Sanya, on the very day Aaraj was born, was Shiva's way of showing him that he is always there, watching, blessing, and guiding.

His ways may surprise us. *His* answers often come in unexpected forms, shaping our lives beyond our understanding. But one thing remains certain:

When Shiva gives, he does not hold back. His love is infinite, and His grace boundless. You cannot thank Him enough—for He does not just fulfil wishes; He showers us with more than we ever thought possible, reminding us that we are never alone.

Key Takeaway: *Divine blessings often come unexpectedly, reaffirming that we are seen, guided, and loved. Recognising these moments deepens our faith and strengthens our connection with the divine.*

Chapter 19

The Nandi Connection

To Aaraj, Shiva is not just a deity—*He* is his Guru, his teacher, his father, his eternal guide. *He* is the formless essence of existence itself, the silent force that shapes his journey. And at the heart of his devotion to Shiva is Nandi—*His* most loyal companion, *His* first disciple, and the very embodiment of unwavering faith.

Nandi, often depicted as a bull, is not just Shiva's vehicle—he is the gatekeeper of divine wisdom, the purest devotee whose gaze never wavers from his Lord. In every Shiva temple across the world, Nandi sits facing the sanctum, his form etched in stone, his devotion an eternal offering.

Aaraj has always seen himself in Nandi. His surrender, patience, and undying love for Shiva are the qualities Aaraj strives to embody. Just as Nandi stands in stillness before Shiva, awaiting *His* command, so too does Aaraj surrender himself, offering his thoughts, prayers, and very being.

One of the most cherished moments of his temple visits is whispering his deepest sentiments into Nandi's ears. It is said that Nandi, in his devotion, carries these messages straight to Shiva, ensuring that every prayer, every longing, reaches its rightful destination.

There is a sacred comfort in this ritual—a feeling that his words, his unspoken desires, are heard. Beyond that, it reminds him that true devotion is not about grand gestures but about quiet, personal moments of connection.

Each time Aaraj sees Nandi, he whispers the message in his ear for Shiva that:

"Tell him that I love him deeply. I know Shiva knows, but please, tell him again from my side."

Aaraj's love for Shiva is not just felt but etched into his very being. On his left arm, inked into his skin, is an image of Shiva in Nandi's form (NandiShiv)—a symbol of strength and wisdom. The tattoo represents Shiva holding a trident in his right hand, a mark of divine power. And in his left, a book, representing eternal knowledge. This image is not just a tattoo—it is a constant reminder of *His* path, a silent vow to always walk in *His* guidance.

Aaraj's parents initially opposed it, but some devotions demand permanence. Just as Shiva marks his devotees with unseen blessings, Aaraj chose to wear his presence openly, letting it become a part of his existence.

For years, Aaraj wore an Ek Mukhi Rudraksha—a bead sacred to Shiva, symbolising pure consciousness. But after Aaraj was inked, He felt a shift in his connection. The need for external adornments faded. His devotion had found a deeper root—one that no longer needed symbols but thrived in the depths of his being.

Each morning, before stepping into the world, Aaraj adorns his forehead with the *tripund* – three sacred lines of ash or Chandan.

It is a reminder:

→ To burn away attachments, like ashes on a pyre.

→ To stay steadfast in his path, unwavering like Nandi.

→ To seek wisdom in Shiva's silence, rather than in the world's noise.

Every act, prayer, and moment of surrender are not just rituals. They are the fabric of his faith, woven into every breath Aaraj takes.

But Shiva is not bound by rituals alone. To truly walk his path, one must go beyond the motions of worship. Discipline, devotion, and an open heart are the true offerings he seeks.

It is not about mere prayers or chants. It is about walking the path with sincerity, about recognising the whispers of his presence in the moments we least expect.

His signs are always there—

- → In the wind that stills your mind.
- → In the silence that answers your questions.
- → In the lessons hidden in the smallest of moments.

But only those who are truly attuned can hear him. Only those who surrender completely can understand his guidance.

- → True connection with Shiva does not come through routine.
- → It comes through devotion.
- → It comes not through rituals but through understanding.

And the more you surrender, the clearer *His* voice becomes. For Shiva does not just bless—*He* awakens.

Key Takeaway: *Loyalty, patience, and unwavering faith—just as Nandi waits for Shiva, we must trust divine timing. When devotion is pure, guidance and answers come naturally, reinforcing the bond between the seeker and the divine.*

Chapter 20

Joey: A Love Beyond Regret

In the depths of Aaraj's heartache, there is a story about Joey, his beloved golden Labrador. Joey was not just a pet; he was family—a companion whose presence filled Aaraj's life with boundless joy, comfort, and unwavering loyalty.

From the moment he entered his world, their bond was forged in love and silent understanding. Joey was Aaraj's confidant, his shadow, his solace in moments of despair. In his eyes, Aaraj found unconditional love; in his presence, Aaraj discovered the purest form of companionship.

But Joey's departure left a void that words fail to express—an ache that lingers, a sorrow that time refuses to erase.

The day Joey fell ill remains etched in Aaraj's memory with painful clarity. What began as subtle signs of discomfort soon turned into a battle against time—a battle Joey fought bravely, even as Aaraj watched helplessly, consumed by guilt.

And that guilt—it was Aaraj's greatest torment.

One moment, one action, one mistake—it changed everything.

In a moment of frustration, blinded by impatience, Aaraj lashed out at Joey. A single strike of a stick. A fleeting action, yet its consequences weighed upon him like an unbearable burden. Joey showed no outward signs of injury, but Aaraj could tell he was deeply hurt internally. It was Joey's fault. Aaraj was angry with him for running off alone on the road—it was dangerous— but Aaraj didn't realise how much he hurt him when he lashed out.

Aaraj never imagined that this moment-this instant of anger and weakness—would become a wound he could never undo.

When the veterinary doctor gave up on Joey and his condition worsened, so did Aaraj's torment. Joey's pain became his mirror, reflecting the depth of his remorse. Aaraj longed to turn back time, to take back that moment, to replace it with love instead of anger.

But regret does not heal wounds. It only deepens them.

As Joey's suffering grew unbearable, Aaraj turned to Bhagwan Shiva, the only one who could understand the turmoil in his soul.

Aaraj pleaded through tears, through shattered prayers—

"Why must he suffer this pain, Shiva?
Take it all—give it to me instead.
I cannot bear to see him in pain,
For it was my hand that caused it.
Forgive me.
Take his soul into your arms,
and grant him the peace I failed to give."

And in that moment, Shiva answered.

Aaraj watched as if held in the stillness of eternity as Joey's soul slipped away—gentle, peaceful, free.

Joey's suffering had ended. He had returned to the infinite, where pain no longer existed.

In the wake of his passing, Aaraj was forced to confront himself—his imperfections, flaws, and frailty as a human being.

Yet, amidst the sorrow, a glimmer of redemption emerged. Joey, even in his departure, had given him his final gift—a lesson in compassion, humility, and the true meaning of unconditional love. His love had never wavered, not even in his last moments. If he could forgive, then surely, Aaraj had to learn to forgive himself.

Joey no longer walks beside him, but he lives on—

- → In the quiet corners of his heart,
- → In the lessons, he taught Aaraj,
- → In the love that still lingers, untouched by time.

And perhaps, somewhere beyond the realms of sorrow and regret, he waits for him—tail wagging, eyes full of love—just as he always did.

Key Takeaway: *We repeat mistakes when we don't learn from them. Recognising patterns is the first step to breaking free. Love, once given, never truly fades—it transforms. Regret teaches us the value of presence, reminding us to cherish the moments we have with those we love before they become memories.*

Chapter 21

From Grief to Redemption: The Arrival of Caesar

In the wake of Joey's departure, his heart remained heavy with grief and guilt, burdened by the unanswered question: Did Aaraj even deserve the love of another pet?

Each day passed in a haze of sorrow and self-reproach. Not a moment went by when Aaraj didn't think of him. To him, Joey was like Shiva in a physical form—pure, loving, unwavering in *His* presence. Losing him felt like losing a part of his soul.

Then, on his sister's birthday, fate intervened.

Amidst the laughter and celebrations, her friends arrived with an unexpected gift—a golden Labrador puppy—a symbol of renewal and a beacon of hope.

Yet, as Aaraj watched the little one play, his heart wrestled with conflicting emotions.

Aaraj wanted to embrace him, to let love in again. But deep inside, a voice whispered:

"You don't deserve this. You failed, Joey. You are not worthy of another pet."

Torn between longing and guilt, as usual, Aaraj turned to Bhagwan Shiva, his eternal refuge.

Through whispers of prayer, Aaraj sought clarity, desperately asking:

"Why another puppy, Shiva?
I do not deserve him.
It was because of me that Joey suffered.
How can I accept this gift when my heart is still heavy with remorse?"

But this time, there was no immediate answer.

No divine whisper, no sudden realisation. Only silence.

Still lost in his turmoil, Aaraj sought distraction on the silver screen—anything to escape the thoughts looping endlessly in his mind.

That evening, Aaraj found himself watching "Rise of the Planet of the Apes." It was a fictional, unrelated movie, yet it would become the medium through which Shiva spoke to him.

In one crucial moment, James Franco's character searches desperately for Caesar, his beloved ape, torn between wanting to protect him and the harsh realities of the world.

As he calls out, Caesar emerges from the shadows—stronger, changed, but still the same at heart. And then, with quiet certainty, he speaks:

"Caesar is home."

In that moment, something within Aaraj shifted.

It was as if Shiva had finally answered him, not through words but meaning. It's Joey who has returned to Aaraj's home!

Caesar had returned not because of the past but because of love. His presence was not about mistakes or failures—it was about a bond that transcended them.

And just like that, Aaraj understood.

This new puppy was not a replacement. He was not a test.

He was a chance. A second chance.

With a deep breath, Aaraj let go of his guilt and held the puppy close.

Aaraj named him Caesar, not just after the character but as a reminder of resilience, love, and the truth that every soul deserves redemption.

With each passing day, Caesar became more than just a pet. He became a symbol of healing, of forgiveness, of Shiva's unspoken grace.

His playful antics, boundless affection, and simple joy reminded him that the past does not define us.

That Shiva does not leave us trapped in guilt.

Shiva does not judge. *He* transforms.

And when we surrender our regrets sincerely, he leads us back into the light.

Today, as Caesar (11 years old now) stands by his side, a cherished member of their family, Aaraj knows one thing for certain:

→ Shiva never abandoned Aaraj.

→ Shiva simply waited for Aaraj to accept the love he thought he didn't deserve.

Key Takeaway: *Healing often comes in unexpected forms. The arrival of Caesar symbolises how love, companionship, and divine intervention can help transform grief into a renewed sense of purpose and redemption.*

Chapter 22

The Dance of Divine Grace

There comes a moment in the journey of devotion when the boundaries between seeker and bestower dissolve, and one realises that Bhagwan Shiva is not merely an observer but an active force within one's life.

It is a sacred shift—from asking to receiving, from longing to gratitude. The ceaseless prayers, the whispered desires, the silent hopes—all fade into a deeper knowing—a realisation that Shiva does not just listen; *He* anticipates.

Shiva does not just give; *He* orchestrates.

Like a tender whisper in the soul's ear, Shiva weaves *His* desires into existence with a precision beyond explanation. *His* grace manifests in ways both grand and simple—sometimes as a lifelong dream fulfilled, other times as a seemingly trivial yet deeply cherished moment.

There have been countless instances where Aaraj's unspoken wishes have effortlessly unfolded before him, as if life itself conspired to bring them to fruition.

→ A sudden craving for a dish, only to find it waiting for him at the dinner table.

→ A silent wish to work in a particular place—only to see the path open before him, effortlessly, unmistakably.

→ A passing thought, a fleeting hope—met with an answer before the question was even formed.

→ A yearning desire to own a dream vehicle and then finally owning it with the bare minimum effort.

These are not coincidences. They are the echoes of a divine presence, a testament to a connection so deep that words are no longer needed.

Shiva's blessings do not always come in an instant. Some unfold like a lightning strike—sudden, dazzling, undeniable. Others take their time, like the slow unfurling of petals in the first light of dawn.

But in every instance, his hand is there, guiding, shaping, aligning.

And then there are the gifts that arrive unannounced—the ones Aaraj never explicitly asked for yet longed for in the depths of his heart. The unexpected surprises, the quiet miracles, the moments when Aaraj is left in awe of how perfectly everything has aligned without him even realising it needed to.

These are the moments that reveal the true magic of devotion.

Each morning, as Aaraj steps into the unknown, he does so with a heart brimming with gratitude.

For Aaraj, do not walk alone. Shiva walks beside him.

His presence is woven into every moment, *His* love manifests in every blessing—seen and unseen, expected and unexpected.

And so, Aaraj surrenders to this eternal dance of devotion—where the seeker and the divine move as one, where faith transforms into experience, and where love transcends the boundaries of time itself.

Key Takeaway: Life unfolds in a rhythmic flow guided by divine grace. When we surrender to Shiva's will, we begin to see how every moment, whether joyful or challenging, is a step in the cosmic dance leading us toward growth and enlightenment.

Chapter 23

Attuning to Shiva's Will

Through love and unwavering devotion, Aaraj has forged a connection so deep that he can sense Shiva's presence, *moods, and* silent guidance. It is a relationship not built on mere rituals but on understanding—a sacred dialogue where *His* will reveals itself through the currents of Aaraj's life.

When Aaraj's desires are pure—untainted by selfish intent—Shiva responds with a swiftness that feels almost effortless. Paths open, opportunities align, and wishes manifest as if the universe itself conspires in harmony with his soul's longing. In these moments, Aaraj knows that Shiva smiles upon him, his grace flowing freely, affirming that he walks the right path.

But not every desire unfolds as Aaraj expects. Sometimes, doors close, obstacles arise, and life takes an unforeseen turn.

In these moments, Aaraj does not question Shiva – he questions himself.

Is my intent truly selfless? Am I walking the path of dharma? Have my actions strayed from righteousness?

Shiva's blessings are never random; they reflect the purity of his heart, the sincerity of his devotion, and the alignment of his karmas. When things do not go his way, Aaraj pauses—not to lament but to reflect, knowing that *His* wisdom often manifests through life's redirections.

Even in uncertainty, Shiva speaks. *His* answers come not as loud proclamations but as whispers in the wind, patterns in life's unfolding, signs in the smallest of moments.

→ A chance encounter.

→ A line in a book.

→ A dream that lingers upon waking.

→ A social media post on Instagram or X.

→ A dialogue from a speaker and more.

Each is a thread in the divine network *Shiva* weaves for Aaraj, guiding him, nudging him, ensuring that he does not drift too far from his purpose. *His* presence is not in grand miracles but in the quiet, persistent ways *He* shapes Aaraj's path.

As Aaraj navigates life's twists and turns, he does so with trust. Not every answered prayer is a blessing, and not every unanswered one is a denial. Some lessons must be learned before gifts can be received.

But through it all, one truth remains—Aaraj is never alone.

For in every breath, in every heartbeat, Shiva walks with him. And as long as Aaraj listens, surrenders, and aligns himself with *His* will, he knows that he will always be guided towards the ultimate truth and liberation.

Key Takeaway: *Surrendering to Shiva's will means trusting the divine plan, even when it is unclear. When we align our actions with faith rather than resistance, we find clarity, purpose, and inner peace.*

Chapter 24

The Transformative Power of Forgiveness and Empathy

Forgiveness is a force of liberation, breaking the chains of resentment and opening the doors to healing and growth. It transforms not just relationships but also the way we perceive ourselves and our journey. As Aaraj reflects on his evolution as a Graphic Designer, He sees how forgiveness, rooted in empathy, has shaped his path in ways he never expected.

His journey into design was far from straightforward. In 11th grade, Aaraj was caught between his parents' differing aspirations for him—his father advocated for science, while his mother leaned towards Commerce, influenced by his maternal uncles' careers. Yet, deep inside, neither felt like his calling. Aaraj struggled with uncertainty, torn between expectations and his own unspoken desires.

This inner conflict persisted through graduation. At his father's insistence, Aaraj enrolled in the Company Secretary of India (ICSI) course, hoping it would provide direction. But the rigid structure of the course suffocated him, making him question his choices. Aaraj remembered asking himself:

"What will I do? What am I truly good at? Will I ever find the right path?"

Amidst this turmoil, a ray of hope emerged—a design course recommended by his cousin Raju. Intrigued, Aaraj embraced creativity with open arms, discovering that design was far more than aesthetics or function; it was a philosophy rooted in empathy.

Graphic Design, Aaraj realised, was about understanding and advocating for the perspectives of others—a principle that resonated deeply with Shiva's wisdom on seeing beyond the self. Every project became an exercise in stepping into another's world, feeling their challenges, and crafting solutions that spoke to their needs.

Beyond his professional journey, Shiva's teachings on perspectives extended into his personal life. There were moments of betrayal, disappointment, and hurt—times when resentment felt justified. But Shiva's wisdom guided him to view these experiences through a different lens.

Instead of holding onto anger, Aaraj asked himself:

"What if I saw this from the other person's perspective? What if I chose to understand rather than condemn?"

It was through empathy—cultivated in his work as a designer—that Aaraj learned the true nature of forgiveness. Forgiveness was not just about absolving others; it was a journey of self-liberation. By shifting his perspective, Aaraj freed himself from the burden of past wounds, allowing healing and renewal to take their place.

Today, as Aaraj looks back, he sees how design and devotion intertwine. The same empathy that helps him craft meaningful designs also helps him navigate life's challenges with wisdom and grace.

Empathy is the thread that connects us to our users, our loved ones, and the divine. It is the key to understanding, the foundation of forgiveness, and the path to true fulfilment.

As Aaraj moves forward, both as a designer and as a devotee of Shiva, he carries this profound lesson with him:

→ To forgive is to set yourself free.

→ To see through the eyes of another is to truly understand.

→ And in understanding, we find both our purpose and our peace.

Key Takeaway: *Forgiveness is not about excusing others but about freeing ourselves from the weight of resentment. Empathy allows us to see beyond our own pain, fostering healing and deeper spiritual growth.*

Chapter 25

The Canvas of Life: Design and Destiny

Life is a grand canvas, where every experience, emotion, and sensation is a deliberate stroke of design. From the radiant hues of a sunset to the rhythmic melody of birdsong, the world is a masterpiece—carefully orchestrated to evoke emotions, shape perceptions, and stir the soul.

Now, imagine a blank white screen—empty, untouched. In this vast openness, every sight, sound, and moment becomes a brushstroke, painting the reality we perceive. This is the essence of design—not just an aesthetic pursuit but a profound force that shapes how we experience the world.

Design is more than form and function; it is the art of crafting experiences. A smartphone, for instance, is not merely an assembly of sleek materials and cutting-edge technology. It is an experience, designed to be intuitive, engaging, and seamless, ensuring that every interaction feels effortless. But design doesn't stop at products; it permeates everything—from the flow of a city's streets to the arrangement of a book's pages. It is the silent architect of human experience.

Yet, while design transforms the external world, it also has the power to shape the internal landscape. This is where Shiva's wisdom enters Aaraj's journey, revealing deeper truths hidden within his path.

Shiva, the eternal source of wisdom, has guided him towards design for a reason. At the time, Aaraj had no idea why, but looking back, Aaraj sees that destiny was unfolding precisely as it was meant to. Design became his medium of self-discovery, a tool through which Aaraj learned to observe, understand, and empathise.

Shiva's teachings go beyond creativity; they are lessons in life itself. *He* has shown that true mastery is not about controlling external circumstances but refining the self. Take anger, for example—a primal force that can cloud judgement and disrupt harmony. Shiva teaches that gaining control over it is an art in itself, one that strengthens not just the mind but the soul. Just as a designer carefully selects and refines each element to create balance, we too must sculpt our thoughts and emotions with mindfulness.

With time, Shiva unveiled the deeper purpose behind his path. *He* taught him empathy—the ability to step into others' shoes, to see the world through their eyes. This lesson became the foundation of his approach to design, influencing not just his work but his interactions with people.

Shiva knows our strengths long before we do. *He* walks beside us, guiding us towards our true potential. And when we surrender to his wisdom, he shapes us, not just as professionals, but as human beings.

Today, as Aaraj designs experiences for others, He realises that he, too, is being designed—moulded by Shiva's unseen hand. Every challenge, every moment of growth, is another stroke on the grand canvas of his life. And with each passing day, Aaraj trusts the process more, knowing that the masterpiece is still unfolding.

***

Key Takeaway: Life is a blend of destiny and personal choices, much like an artist painting on a predefined canvas. While certain events are predetermined, how we navigate them, the colours we choose, and the strokes we make define our unique journey.

Chapter 26

Lessons from the Bosses

In the ever-evolving world of corporate life, the influence of bosses extends far beyond professional growth—it shapes character, resilience, and perspective. Over Aaraj's 20-year+ career across three companies, he had the privilege of working under four distinct industry leaders. Each left an indelible mark, not just on his career but on his understanding of leadership, empowerment, and personal transformation. Looking back, Aaraj sees that their guidance echoes Bhagwan Shiva's wisdom, teaching him lessons that extended beyond the workplace.

Gautam: The Creative Force
During their approximately four years together, Gautam embodied creativity, hard work, resilience, and humility. He challenged conventional thinking, pushing Aaraj to embrace innovation and push boundaries. Under his guidance, Aaraj learned that perseverance in the face of obstacles is not just a professional necessity—it is a way

of life. His lessons became the pillars of his work ethic, reinforcing the importance of continuous improvement.

Manoj: The Trust Builder

With a decade-long mentorship, Manoj became his gateway to mastery in Design. His expertise was unparalleled, but what truly set him apart was his ability to instil trust and grant freedom. He created an environment where creativity flourished, where individuals felt empowered to take ownership of their work. From him, Aaraj learned that true leadership lies in allowing others to grow, in fostering autonomy rather than control.

Jaideep: The Strategic Visionary

During their two years together, Jaideep sharpened Aaraj's understanding of strategy and communication. He taught him that clarity of thought and foresight are essential for success. His meticulous approach to planning showed him the importance of aligning daily efforts with long-term objectives. Under his mentorship, Aaraj refined his ability to articulate ideas succinctly, ensuring that vision translated into action.

Shalil: The Master Persuader

Over three years, Shalil demonstrated the power of influence and persuasion. He was not just a communicator; he was a force of inspiration. Watching him, Aaraj understood that true leadership is not about authority but about connection—about inspiring people through authenticity and empathy. From him, Aaraj learned the art of storytelling in leadership, the ability to move hearts and minds with conviction and purpose.

It is often said that bosses can either build or break careers. Insecure leaders create toxicity, but those secure in their wisdom uplift and nurture. Aaraj was fortunate to learn from leaders who empowered rather than constrained, who mentored rather than dictated. Looking back, Aaraj sees Shiva's grace in this journey. *He* placed him under the guidance of individuals who shaped his path, preparing him for his own evolution.

Shiva, the supreme teacher, has always been by his side through every challenge, lesson, and milestone. *His* presence taught him that true leadership is not about control but about empowerment. It is about elevating those around you, just as Shiva lifts his devotees with wisdom and strength.

As Aaraj reflects on his journey, he realises that his bosses were more than mentors; they were instruments of divine learning. Through them, Aaraj discovered resilience, trust, vision, and influence—qualities that extend far beyond the workplace. As Aaraj continues on this path, he does so with gratitude, knowing that every challenge and every leader was placed in his life for a reason, as part of a grander design—Shiva's design.

Key Takeaway: *Every leader, whether good or challenging, teaches us valuable lessons. Some inspire growth, while others test our patience and resilience. The key is to absorb wisdom from every experience and use it to shape our journey with strength and humility.*

Chapter 27

The Weight of Leadership

Leadership is a privilege, but it comes with its burdens, especially when tough decisions must be made. In the corporate world, where financial pressures dictate choices, leaders often find themselves at a crossroads, forced to balance business needs with human impact.

Throughout his career, Aaraj has faced these dilemmas firsthand. Cost-cutting measures and restructuring are sometimes inevitable, yet they carry profound consequences. While Aaraj has been fortunate to remain on the safe side of such decisions, he has witnessed their effects on colleagues and felt the moral weight of making those calls.

Decisions about who stays and who goes are often made behind closed doors, known only to a select few. As someone who holds deep faith and values, Aaraj has wrestled with the morality of these choices. Even when his hands are tied, he finds himself seeking forgiveness and guidance, knowing that these decisions, though difficult, shape real lives.

One moment still lingers in his mind. A team member, feeling overwhelmed, requested a transfer to another department. Aaraj advocated for him, but circumstances beyond his control led to his exit. The fact that it happened during a period of financial scrutiny and cost optimisation only deepened his sense of helplessness.

In moments like these, Aaraj turns to Bhagwan Shiva, seeking clarity and reassurance. He reminds himself that every action is accounted for in the balance of karma and that leadership is not about avoiding difficult decisions—it is about making them with integrity and compassion. Shiva's watchful gaze reminds him that as long as his intentions are pure, he must trust the larger plan at play.

Despite the pressures, his commitment remains unwavering—to lead with fairness, uplift his team, and make even the toughest choices with a heart that remains human. High performance is expected, but Aaraj strives to create an environment where people feel valued and empowered.

True leadership is not about being perfect. It is about making the hardest decisions with honesty, fairness, and faith. In the ever-changing tides of corporate life, keeping our moral compass intact is the only way to emerge not just successful, but whole.

Key Takeaway: *Leadership is not just about authority but about responsibility, sacrifice, and making tough decisions. True leaders must balance power with humility, ensuring their actions align with higher values and the greater good.*

Chapter 28

Different Paths, Same Light

In the dynamic world of corporate life, where diverse personalities collide, Aaraj's two colleagues—Ved and Sawan—find themselves bound not just by professional responsibilities but by a deeper connection: their shared devotion to Bhagwan Shiva. Evidently, Aaraj got connected to both of them. Yet, despite their equal faith, their perspectives on work and life could not be more different.

Ved sees the world through the lens of unwavering principles. Guided by Shiva's teachings, they believe in integrity, righteousness, and a duty-driven approach. For Ved, every task—no matter how small—is infused with spiritual significance, a form of worship in itself.

Sawan, too, is deeply devoted to Shiva, but his approach is more pragmatic. He navigates the corporate landscape with adaptability, flexibility, and a focus on results. While faith remains central to Sawan's life, he believes in adjusting to circumstances, trusting that Shiva's wisdom is found in both strategy and surrender.

Ved and Sawan often clash in their views, each convinced of their righteousness. Their debates raise an eternal question:

"If two people share the same devotion and passion, why do they see the world so differently? Why does fate favour one path over another?"

Through their interactions, Aaraj begins to see that devotion does not demand uniformity—Shiva's wisdom manifests in multiple ways.

The universe thrives on duality: day and night, stillness and motion, detachment and engagement. Ved and Sawan represent two sides of the same truth—one rooted in steadfastness, the other in fluidity.

Corporate life can be unpredictable—difficult colleagues, office politics, and unexpected setbacks. Yet, Shiva's presence is a constant reminder that true protection lies in integrity, resilience, and karma. Whether one chooses Ved's steadfast path or Sawan's adaptive approach, what truly matters is acting with sincerity and righteousness.

Shiva does not dictate a single way—he empowers us to find our own. In the end, both Ved and Sawan realise that their differences are not divisions but complementary strengths, teaching them that devotion is not about being the same but about honouring the path that resonates with one's soul.

No matter how different our journeys may seem, the light of Shiva illuminates all paths, guiding, protecting, and shaping our destinies in ways we may not always understand.

***Key Takeaway:** All spiritual paths, no matter how different they seem, ultimately lead to the same divine truth. Whether through devotion, wisdom, or service, every seeker is moving toward the same light—Shiva's eternal presence.*

Chapter 29

The Power of Persistence

Where dreams shimmer like distant stars, there exists a timeless wisdom whispered by sages and seekers alike:

Persistence paves the path to fruition.

It is a mantra that reverberates through the corridors of time, resonating with the unwavering resolve of those who dare to tread the solitary road of devotion.

For Aaraj, this mantra finds its essence in unwavering dedication to Bhagwan Shiva, the harbinger of strength and solace amidst the tumult of existence.

His devotion to Shiva hinges on a single principle:

Persistence.

It is the steadfast commitment to a chosen path, regardless of the trials and tribulations that may beset the journey.

Yet, in this journey of persistence, there exists a myriad of distractions, lurking like shadows in the recesses of the mind. Evil spirits, contrary thoughts, and the seductive allure of materialism conspire to derail one's motives and sow seeds of doubt along the way. The path of devotion becomes fraught with obstacles, testing the resilience of one's resolve at every turn.

"I am not God; mistakes are bound to happen. Why do you always want to punish me for even the smallest mistakes? Why can't I be forgiven for these minor wrongdoings when no one is getting hurt because of me?"

Aaraj recalls countless instances where the siren song of distraction beckoned, tempting him to stray from the righteous path. In moments of weakness, doubts gnawed at the edges of his conviction, threatening to overshadow the beacon of faith that guided his steps. Yet, like a ship navigating treacherous waters, Aaraj clung to the mast of his devotion, weathering the storm with unwavering resolve.

But alas, Aaraj is not immune to the frailties of human nature. There have been times when he faltered, when the allure of shortcuts and the whispers of temptation led him astray. Each misstep filled him with remorse and regret, akin to the pang of guilt that accompanies a breach of trust in matters of the heart.

How could I betray the trust of Shiva, the ever watchful witness to my deeds?

Yet, amidst the shadows of failure, there shines a beacon of hope: the unwavering presence of Shiva. *He* stands as a pillar of strength and forgiveness in the face of human frailty. Despite his shortcomings, Shiva remains steadfast in his love and compassion, offering infinite chances to redeem himself and prove his worthiness.

It is this unwavering support that fuels his determination to persevere, to rise from the ashes of failure and strive once more towards the lofty ideals set forth by Shiva. Failures may test his resolve, but they do not define him. Each setback serves as a poignant reminder of the distance yet to be traversed on the path of devotion.

As Aaraj gazes towards the horizon, he envisions a future where distractions hold no sway over his steadfast resolve. A future where Aaraj walks hand in hand with Shiva, unwavering in his commitment to follow the path of righteousness. It is a journey fraught with challenges, but one that promises the ultimate reward: the fulfilment of Shiva's expectations and the realisation of his true potential.

In the end, it is not the destination that defines the journey, but the unwavering commitment to persevere in the face of adversity. And so, Aaraj marches onward, guided by the light of Shiva's love, ever mindful of the path that lies ahead and the promise of fulfilment that awaits those who dare to persist.

Shiva does not expect perfection; he values persistence. As long as we continue walking his path, despite our stumbles, we remain under his divine protection.

Key Takeaway: *Success and spiritual growth are not achieved overnight; they require unwavering dedication and patience. By staying committed to our path, despite obstacles, we align with divine timing and ultimately reach our destined goals.*

Chapter 30

Why people can't find Shiva

Woven with threads of faith and devotion, the mysteries of divine blessings often confound the mind and stir the soul. Questions linger like shadows, seeking answers that elude even the most fervent seekers. Such is the nature of his journey as a devotee of Bhagwan Shiva, where the unfolding of his grace is both profound and perplexing.

Growing up alongside Aaraj's sister, Poorvi, both of them deeply devoted to Shiva, Aaraj often pondered the disparities in their journeys.

How is it that I achieved success while she struggled in her endeavours? Why did fortune smile upon me—a Product of a humble government school—while my friend Ashish, who had the advantage of private education, faltered?

These questions gnawed at his mind, casting doubts upon the nature of divine blessings. If devotion to

Shiva is the key, why do two equally faithful individuals experience such different fates?

The contrast between his experiences and those of his friends or his sister left him searching for answers.

"Why was I able to grasp the intricacies of my dreams and interpret their hidden meanings, while others remained adrift in uncertainty? How is it that I found a life partner who embodied the qualities I sought, while others wandered in search of elusive companionship?"

Such questions, born from deep introspection, led him to seek solace and guidance from Bhagwan Shiva. Aaraj turned to him, yearning for clarity and understanding. The journey was often confusing, filled with moments where his own devotion seemed at odds with the reality of the world around him.

For years, Aaraj traversed the conflicting paths of his own existence, stumbling yet never losing sight of Shiva's guiding light. Through these trials, Aaraj learned an invaluable lesson: perseverance.

Like a pilgrim navigating treacherous terrain, Aaraj faced obstacles that tested the limits of his resolve. Yet, with unwavering faith in Shiva's guidance, Aaraj pressed onward. Each setback became a stepping stone, bringing him closer to the truths Aaraj sought.

The more he trusted in Shiva, the more he realised that divine blessings are not merely handed to us – they must be uncovered through devotion, effort, and patience.

It was in moments of quiet introspection—amidst life's chaos—that Aaraj began to unravel the enigma of divine blessings. Through prayer and contemplation, he unearthed truths that had long eluded him. The answers, once obscured by his own limited understanding, became clear as day, illuminating the path before him.

In the end, it was not luck or chance that led him to Shiva's grace, but a steadfast commitment to follow the path set before him. Through unwavering devotion and relentless perseverance, Aaraj forged a connection with the divine that transcended mortal understanding.

As Aaraj reflects upon his journey, he is reminded of the wisdom passed down through the ages:

"Seek, and you shall find. Ask, and it shall be given unto you."

Divine blessings are not bestowed without effort. We must seek them with open hearts, attuned minds, and unwavering faith. Only then do we begin to understand the deeper mysteries of Shiva's grace.

And so, Aaraj continues on his journey, guided by Shiva's love and wisdom. Though the answers may not always be immediate, he takes solace in knowing that with faith, devotion, and perseverance, all shall be revealed in due time.

Key Takeaway: *Shiva's presence is felt by those who seek Him with an open heart and a surrendered mind. Many fail to recognise Him because they are entangled in doubts, material distractions, or rigid perceptions. True connection comes through faith, awareness, and an inner calling.*

Chapter 31

The Weight of Comparisons from Fellow Shiva Devotees

Comparison is an intrinsic part of human nature, shaping our aspirations and fuelling our insecurities. From childhood self-doubts to professional ambitions, it often dictates our perception of success and failure. Yet, when it seeps into the realm of spiritual devotion, its impact becomes far more profound. Among fellow Shiva devotees, each walking their own sacred path, comparison can stir emotions of inadequacy, questioning why some appear more blessed while others endure relentless hardships.

Among the many souls who have illuminated Aaraj's spiritual journey, his uncle, Yash, stands as a paragon of virtue. His unwavering faith in good karma, his kindness, and his steadfast devotion to Shiva serve as a benchmark that humbles him during his childhood. His quiet strength is a constant reminder of the discipline true devotion demands.

Similarly, his sister Poorvi's boundless reverence for Shiva mirrors her selflessness. Yet, despite her deep faith and pure heart, she faces endless struggles. Observing her hardships, Aaraj has often found himself pondering the enigmatic workings of destiny. If devotion were measured by piety alone, shouldn't she be showered with divine grace?

As Aaraj looks around at fellow Shiva bhakts, Aaraj sees a mosaic of unwavering faith interwoven with trials:

- Tony embarks on his annual Kawar Yatra, carrying sacred water with unshaken determination.

- Ved makes pilgrimages to Kedarnath, seeking Shiva's blessings.

- Sawan inscribes his devotion on his skin; his body is a canvas of reverence.

- Suvrajit feels a divine calling, drawn inexplicably to Shiva's path.

- Neeraj turns to Shiva for guidance in times of doubt and uncertainty.

- Poorvi, despite her ceaseless chants and unyielding faith, faces adversity that raises questions about the justice of fate.

Each of them has found a way to express their devotion, yet their faith does not shield them from suffering. Their stories paint a poignant picture of divine devotion entwined with personal trials.

The paradox of devotion and suffering is most evident in those closest to Aaraj:

→ Poorvi's altruism contrasts sharply with her unrelenting struggles.

→ Sawan, always cheerful, hides the deep scars of a painful divorce.

→ Ved, who cherishes his father, carries the grief of irreparable loss.

→ Neeraj, embodying warmth and love, still awaits a life partner despite his kindness.

Each of them reminds him that Shiva's ways are often beyond human comprehension. Their pain and perseverance teach him that devotion does not promise immunity from hardships. Instead, it grants the strength to withstand the storms.

Through their experiences, Aaraj has come to realise that Shiva's teachings manifest not only in triumph but also in tribulation. Every obstacle, every unanswered prayer, and every moment of despair serves a higher purpose. Their paths may appear different, but they are all sculpting us into stronger, wiser beings.

Comparison is a natural tendency, but it often blinds us to a deeper truth—that everything happens for our ultimate good. We question why others seem to have more, why our efforts don't yield the same results, or whether we are somehow less deserving. But Shiva, in his wisdom, gives us exactly what we need, when we need it.

Even when we walk the same path, our destinies unfold uniquely, shaped by our karma, persistence, and the lessons we must learn. The journey is not about having more or less, but about how we evolve through trials and experiences.

Shiva remains the guiding force, ensuring that every challenge, every delay, and every blessing serve a purpose in our growth. Trust *His* timing. Trust *His* ways.

Key Takeaway: *Spiritual journeys are unique, and comparison only hinders personal growth. True devotion is measured by an inner connection with Shiva, not by external rituals or societal validation.*

Chapter 32

A Question That Stirred The Soul

There are moments when our deepest beliefs collide with the perceptions of those closest to us. Such was the case when Jane questioned why Aaraj incessantly spoke of Bhagwan Shiva, attributing every success and blessing to his divine presence. Her words struck a chord within him, prompting deep reflection.

Aaraj realised that his devotion to Shiva was not merely a matter of choice but an inseparable part of his identity. It was not about habit or ritual—it was the essence of who Aaraj was. Every milestone, every blessing, every moment of strength Aaraj had experienced was, in his heart, a testament to his divine presence.

"I am not seeking validation from anyone. When I give all the credit to Shiva for my life's success, I truly mean it. Why does anyone doubt my intentions when I credit Him for all the good in me?"

Aaraj recalled countless instances where Shiva's guidance had steered him through life's challenges.

From moments of despair when all seemed lost to triumphs that defied logic, *His* hand had been the unseen force behind his resilience. Whether it was finding the courage to chase his dreams or navigating relationships, *His* wisdom illuminated his path.

Yet, the tangible world often struggles to recognise the intangible power of faith. Jane's scepticism was a reminder of that divide—she saw his devotion as an exaggeration, while Aaraj knew it to be the very foundation of his being. To him, there was no separation between the sacred and the mundane; every moment was infused with his divine presence.

Aaraj tried to make her understand—his reverence for Shiva was not about seeking validation or recognition. It was not a performance. It was a truth that pulsed through his veins. *He* was the silent force behind every decision, every action, every bit of wisdom that guided his life.

Despite her reservations, Aaraj hoped she would see that his devotion was not a barrier between them, but a pillar of strength. Aaraj could no more cease to speak of *Him* than he could cease to breathe, for Shiva was the very breath of life within him.

As Aaraj spoke, he sensed a shift in her demeanour—a softening, a flicker of understanding behind the veil of doubt. Perhaps, in time, she would realise that his faith was not a cause for contention but a source of deep inner peace.

In the end, Aaraj resolved to continue on his path, unashamed and unwavering in his devotion. He would proclaim the glory of Bhagwan Shiva at every opportunity, not to convince the world, but because his soul demanded it. In *His* presence, Aaraj found purpose, meaning, and fulfilment beyond measure.

Though others may question or doubt, his faith remains steadfast – an unshakeable beacon of light amidst the uncertainties of the world.

Key Takeaway: *Some questions shake us to our core, forcing deep introspection. Instead of fearing them, embracing these questions can lead to profound self-discovery and a stronger connection with the divine.*

Chapter 33

The Guiding Light

Belief serves as a guiding light, illuminating the path forward amidst the uncertainties that surround us. For Aaraj, this unwavering belief finds its anchor in the divine presence of Shiva—a source of solace and strength that transcends human understanding. While many seek comfort in the love and support of family, friends, or partners, his journey has been one of solitary reliance on Shiva. *His* presence is not merely a theological concept but an ever-present force, providing an unshakeable sanctuary of reassurance and peace.

Though his family's love is boundless, it pales in comparison to the depth of devotion Aaraj feels towards Shiva. His love is indefinable yet profoundly real, a presence that comforts him in moments of turmoil—especially in the quiet hours before sleep, when self-doubt and reflection often arise. Despite his professional confidence, Aaraj struggles with insecurities on a personal level. His spouse, progressive and ambitious, sets high expectations (but rightly so), and at times,

Aaraj feels inadequate in meeting them. Yet, amid these challenges, his commitment to his daughter's well-being remains steadfast. Sanya is his grounding force, reminding him that love, in its purest form, must rise above ego and self-doubt.

As Aaraj observes the struggles of others, he sees how ego, insecurities, and unresolved traumas create barriers in relationships. The complexities of human interactions, the unspoken pain, and the weight of expectations often lead to conflict and despair.

Why do people succumb to self-harm or allow pride to fracture relationships? Why do people commit suicide?

These questions often linger in his mind, reminding him that every soul carries its burden, and healing requires patience and faith.

It is Shiva's love that guides him back to the light. *His* presence is not just a belief but a tangible force that lifts him out of uncertainty and fear. *He* whispers courage into his heart, challenging him to confront his insecurities, to trust in his divine plan, and to surrender his burdens at *His* feet.

Shiva's love is not conditional – it does not waver with his doubts or falter in his weakest moments. Instead, it remains an eternal beacon, reminding him that true strength lies in surrendering to the divine and embracing faith over fear.

Life's complexities often test our faith, but in Shiva's love, Aaraj finds the resilience to face adversity. *His* wisdom teaches him that every challenge is a lesson, every struggle a step towards spiritual growth. In surrendering to *His* will, Aaraj discovers the courage to overcome his inner demons and emerge stronger, ready to embrace the path *He* has laid out for him.

Ultimately, it is Shiva's unconditional love that sustains him. It is a love that does not require validation, explanation, or justification. It simply exists—profound, unwavering, and eternal. In his divine presence, Aaraj finds not only solace but also purpose. No matter the trials ahead, he walks forward with the assurance that he is never alone, for Shiva's love will always be his guiding light.

Key Takeaway: *Shiva's presence is a constant source of strength, guiding us through life's uncertainties. Trusting in His wisdom allows us to find clarity, resilience, and purpose even in the darkest times.*

Chapter 34

The Breaking Point:
A Battle Within

There are moments of unbearable pain, and this day was one of them. Aaraj always tells people not to bottle up their emotions because, like a pressure cooker, they will eventually explode. And that's exactly what happened to him today.

A Heated Argument and an Overflow of Emotion

This morning, a heated argument with Jane left him shaken to the core. In those moments, his entire existence felt questioned.

"I know I'm not perfect—I accept my mistakes—but I'm human, not a saint. I have feelings, too, and there's only so much my mind can take before it overflows. Without an outlet, it bursts."

This pain made him question everything.

"Why isn't Shiva helping me? What does he want from me? Is he punishing me? Am I really at fault for everything?"

Out of frustration, Aaraj punished himself by not eating for the entire day. But in the end, who was really suffering? Not Jane, not anyone else—only him. And deep down, Aaraj knew his fight wasn't with her. It was with Shiva. If *He* is the doer of all things, then why was *He* making him go through this?

As Aaraj sat in his office, lost in these thoughts, a colleague, Manish, suddenly dropped by, literally dragged him to the cafeteria, and made him eat. He shared his meal. Aaraj didn't resist. In that moment, Aaraj gave in—not to him, but to Shiva. Because maybe, just maybe, this was *His* way of intervening.

Life with Shiva is like a rollercoaster. It's impossible to predict what *He* wants from you. But one thing Aaraj knows for sure—Shiva loves him deeply. Ending life is easy, but living through these storms is the real challenge.

On his way to the office after the fight, a thought crossed his mind:

"What if I completely let go? What if I stop caring about anything—family, career, responsibilities? If I walk away, everything will collapse. My family will break, my profession will end, lives will be shattered."

But then, Aaraj surrendered. He said YES to *Him*.

I don't care about the outcome anymore. I'll manage. I don't need money or security. After all, what does money really buy? Just food and shelter. And if that's all, I could live in the wilderness, drink from rivers, and survive on nothing—or beg, like the saints who have given up everything.

Could I Truly Live That Life?

These thoughts sound simple, but could I truly live that life? Could I let go of everything I had built, of everyone who depended on me?

Yet surrender is not a sign of weakness but a testament to the strength of the human spirit. In relinquishing control and placing his trust in Shiva, Aaraj finds solace, strength, and the courage to face whatever challenges lie ahead.

To surrender, you have to let go…

Key Takeaway: Our greatest struggles often come from within. When faced with emotional turmoil and inner conflict, surrendering to Shiva's guidance can help us break free from self-imposed limitations and find strength in acceptance.

Chapter 35

The Art of Letting Go

In the noise of our minds and the chaos of our thoughts, one simple truth remains: most of our stress is self-created. We overthink every situation, weaving endless worries, only to trap ourselves in anxiety. But what if, instead of getting lost in our thoughts, we simply let go and trust Shiva's wisdom?

Growing up, Aaraj often heard the phrase:

"Don't think too much; leave it to God."

But like many, Aaraj brushed it off, not realising the depth of its meaning. It was only through life's struggles that he truly understood the power of surrender.

But letting go isn't easy. Our minds crave control, clinging to worries as if they will somehow change the outcome. In reality, overthinking only increases our stress.

Aaraj learned this the hard way during a particularly stressful time at work. Deadlines piled up, pressure mounted, and he was drowning in anxiety. Every day felt like a battle against his own thoughts.

Exhausted, Aaraj finally surrendered. Instead of micromanaging every detail, he trusted Shiva. The moment he let go, he felt lighter, free from the weight of unnecessary stress.

Surrender isn't something we do once; it's a lifelong practice. It takes patience, faith, and trust. Each time we let go, we move closer to inner peace.

In the grand scheme of life, our struggles are small compared to the vastness of the universe. Our fears and anxieties are fleeting, just shadows passing through time. Yet, in the middle of all this uncertainty, there is a guiding force—Shiva. *He* watches over us with love, whispering to us in moments of doubt.

Shiva teaches us that true freedom doesn't come from controlling everything—it comes from surrendering to something greater. When we release our worries, like leaves carried by the wind, we allow life to unfold as it should.

And in that surrender, we don't just find peace – we discover the freedom to truly live.

Key Takeaway: *Letting go is not about giving up but about freeing yourself from attachments that no longer serve your growth. Surrendering to Shiva's will brings peace, clarity, and the strength to move forward.*

Chapter 36

The Power of Humility

It was another bad day, another heated argument with Jane—ego clashed with ego, threatening to unravel the delicate threads of their relationship. For a moment, Aaraj felt the weight of his pride, the urge to prove himself right. But then, clarity struck. Aaraj chose humility over pride.

He extended an olive branch, offering an apology. Yet, as he walked home, uncertainty lingered—would his gesture make a difference? Aaraj had no way of knowing.

Amidst his inner turmoil, life had another lesson in store for him. Lost in thought, walking back from the grocery store with his daughter Sanya, a sudden honk jolted him back to reality. Before Aaraj could react, a passing car brushed against his right elbow, leaving him stunned. The driver sped away, indifferent to what had just happened.

For a brief moment, anger surged within him. Aaraj had every right to be upset. But as the shock faded, he realised he had a choice—to hold onto resentment or to let it go. Instead of lashing out at the driver, he chose patience. Though his conversation with the driver brought no real closure, Aaraj found peace in the fact that he had chosen understanding over rage.

Still reflecting on the incident, Aaraj absentmindedly scrolled through Twitter. A video post of Amitabh Bachchan (Bollywood actor) caught his attention—he spoke about the difference between confidence and ego.

"Confidence leads us towards success, while ego blinds us to our flaws, pushing us towards destruction."

His words struck a deep chord. At that moment, Aaraj understood the power of humility. No matter the injustices we face, humility allows us to navigate life with grace and dignity. It isn't a weakness—it's a strength.

Shiva's teachings, though often mysterious, guide us when we need them most. Even in our darkest moments, *He* watches over us with love and compassion. We may not always understand *His* ways, but if we listen closely, *His* wisdom is always there.

As Aaraj reflects on today, he realises that life's greatest lessons often come in unexpected ways. Ego builds walls, but humility builds bridges. In conflict, it's easy to let pride take over, to withdraw, or to inflict pain on ourselves—but none of that brings peace.

Surrendering to Shiva doesn't mean giving up; it means trusting that *He* will guide us through even the toughest trials. *He* gives us strength not just to endure, but to grow, heal, and find deeper love and understanding.

When you take a step back and examine the cause of your stress, you often realise that you were wrong all along – or that you had misunderstood the situation. A new perspective can completely change how you feel.

Aaraj wishes he had understood this earlier, but Shiva has been trying to tell him all along:

"Don't think too much. Leave it to me."

And whenever Aaraj surrenders to *Him,* he feels at peace.

Key Takeaway: *Humility is not a sign of weakness but a reflection of inner strength. True power lies in remaining grounded, acknowledging the divine in all, and letting go of ego to embrace spiritual growth.*

Chapter 37

AI vs. Spirituality: Seeking Answers Beyond Data

Artificial intelligence (AI) is reshaping industries and economies at an unprecedented pace, bringing both opportunities and challenges. In India, the world's most populous nation, this rapid technological shift has led to job losses and an urgent need for workers to upskill in order to stay relevant.

As AI continues to advance, corporations focus on retaining high-paid industry leaders while cutting costs through layoffs. Interns and lower-level employees often bear the brunt of these changes, as job security becomes increasingly uncertain. The once-stable employment landscape is shifting, leaving many workers anxious about their future.

A Question of Faith and Technology by Aaraj:

"What can an AI answer that Shiva cannot? If AI can provide fast answers, why do I receive delayed answers

from Shiva? Can AI offer me quick solutions to my personal problems?"

Amid this uncertainty, Aaraj turns to both technology and spirituality for guidance.

AI, with its data-driven precision, offers efficiency and quick answers, but it lacks the depth of human emotions and experiences. On the other hand, faith— such as devotion to Shiva—provides comfort through introspection and spiritual growth, offering a sense of purpose beyond logic and algorithms.

This contrast between AI and spirituality raises thought-provoking questions.

Can technology truly shape human destiny? Can precise, machine-generated answers replace the wisdom gained through faith and reflection?

AI impresses with its accuracy, drawing from vast amounts of data and human-designed algorithms. Yet, for all its intelligence, it remains a tool—one that lacks true understanding of human emotions, struggles, and aspirations.

In contrast, spirituality offers something AI cannot: a sense of transcendence.

Seeking guidance from Shiva has given Aaraj solace in times of uncertainty, helping him trust that a greater force is shaping his path. Unlike AI, which provides definitive answers, spirituality encourages personal interpretation and growth, reminding us that not everything in life has a clear-cut solution.

Aaraj's experiences with both AI and spirituality have also shown him the power of clear communication. AI responds best to precise queries, while spiritual guidance often requires deep reflection and patience. This highlights the importance of being intentional and mindful in how we seek answers, whether from technology or faith.

Ultimately, the rise of AI invites us to reflect on what it means to be human. As we embrace new technologies, we must also consider their ethical and philosophical impact.

True progress lies not just in advancing technology but in balancing it with the wisdom, emotions and deeper understanding that make us who we are.

Key Takeaway: AI enhances human capabilities, but true wisdom and consciousness come from spiritual awakening. While AI processes data, spirituality connects us to divine intelligence beyond logic and algorithms. The real challenge is to balance technological progress with inner growth, ensuring that AI serves humanity without diminishing our spiritual essence.

Chapter 38

From Self-Doubt to Self-Acceptance

In moments of solitude, when the world's noise fades, self-doubt grows louder. It is a familiar shadow, one that has followed him for as long as Aaraj can remember—whispering that he is not good enough. No matter how hard Aaraj tries to silence it, it lingers, like a stain that refuses to fade.

From childhood to adulthood, this feeling of inadequacy has been a constant companion. It sneaks into quiet moments, planting seeds of doubt that take root in his mind.

"Why am I not good enough to make people understand something? Why do I lack strong communication skills or the ability to influence others? Why do I feel unworthy of myself? Why do I feel like I don't have any innate talent that I can be proud of or confidently share with others?"

Aaraj has tried to shake it off, to step into self-assurance. But no matter how hard he tries, the burden of his insecurities feels too heavy to carry alone. They shape how he sees himself and colour his views of the world.

When the weight becomes too much, Aaraj turns to faith. For him, that faith lies in Shiva—a source of strength in the storm. Through prayer and introspection, he seeks comfort in the belief that his journey has a greater purpose, even when the path ahead is unclear.

Yet, even in faith, doubt creeps in.

"You are not worthy," the voices whisper again, trying to drown out hope. It's a battle between light and darkness, between faith and fear. But even in his lowest moments, Aaraj holds on to the small flame of hope, believing that a way forward exists, even when hidden in shadows.

Through this journey, he has learned that overcoming self-doubt isn't about eliminating darkness but embracing the light. It's about recognising our fears, facing them, and choosing to move forward despite them. Even in the darkest nights, a spark of hope can always be found.

Aaraj now understands that worthiness isn't something we have to earn—it is already within us. Our flaws and struggles do not define us; our existence itself is proof that we are enough.

As Aaraj navigates life, he remembers Rumi's words:

"The wound is the place where the light enters you."

His doubts and struggles are not signs of weakness but opportunities for growth. By confronting them, Aaraj opens himself to healing, strength, and transformation.

And so, Aaraj moves forward, one step at a time, knowing that even in his darkest moments, there is always light waiting to guide him home.

Key Takeaway: Self-doubt is a natural part of growth, but true transformation begins when we embrace ourselves fully. Acceptance is not about ignoring flaws but understanding that we are always evolving. Trusting in divine guidance and recognising our worth helps us shift from self-criticism to self-belief, allowing us to walk our path with confidence and peace.

Chapter 39

Destiny vs. Free Will:
Who Really Decides?

Is life already written, or do we shape it with our choices? This question has followed humanity for ages, and like many, Aaraj has wrestled with it himself.

There are days when Aaraj finds comfort in believing everything is preordained and that a higher power has already set the course of his life. And yet, on difficult days—when setbacks feel unfair and challenges seem relentless—he begins to question everything.

Am I just a passenger in this life, or do my choices matter?

On some of those days, the temptation to escape is strong. After years of sobriety, there are moments when an old voice whispers,

What difference does it make? If everything is already written, then why fight it?

But then, something small—almost insignificant—reminds him that life is not just about what happens to us, but also about how we respond.

That morning, like any other, Aaraj was rushing to leave for work. As he reached into his car to grab his lunch bag, he saw his fruit scattered across the floor—a mess caused by his hurried packing. Annoyed, he sighed.

"Why did this happen?"
Was it just bad luck? Or was it something more?

Aaraj found himself questioning it.

"Did I do something wrong this morning? Was I driving too fast? Is Shiva trying to warn me of something?"

Aaraj paused. It felt ridiculous to assign meaning to such a small inconvenience. But then, a thought settled in his mind—calm and clear, as if whispered from somewhere beyond me:

"I told you to place your lunch bag behind your laptop for support."

Aaraj froze. Because the truth was, he had thought about doing that earlier in the morning. A fleeting instinct, quickly ignored.

And there it was – the answer.

He had always believed that fate controlled everything. But in that tiny moment, Shiva reminded him:

Destiny may create circumstances, but our choices shape our experience.

Had Aaraj listened to his instinct and placed the lunch bag correctly, the fruit wouldn't have fallen. It wasn't fate – it was his action, or lack thereof.

Life is like that. We often blame circumstances for our struggles, but many times, the signs were already there. Shiva doesn't just dictate fate; he guides us, nudges us, and whispers wisdom along the way. But it is up to us whether we listen.

That morning, Aaraj realised something profound: Shiva's role is not to control his life but to guide him through it.

→ *He* offers wisdom, but *He* does not force it upon him.

→ *He* shows the way, but Aaraj must choose to walk it.

So, is life written, or do we write it ourselves? The answer is both.

Shiva may place the brush in our hands, but we must choose the colours.

Some things are beyond our control, but in every moment, we have the power to respond—to act with awareness, to listen to our intuition, and to make mindful choices.

And as Aaraj moves forward, he does so with faith, not just in destiny, but in his ability to shape it. Because Shiva's guidance, combined with his choices, will lead him exactly where he is meant to be.

Key Takeaway: *Life is a dynamic interplay between destiny and free will. While destiny sets the stage with predetermined circumstances, our choices shape the journey. Shiva's guidance helps us navigate this balance, showing that surrendering to the divine while making conscious efforts leads to the best outcomes. True wisdom lies in understanding when to act and trust the flow of life.*

Chapter 40

I Don't Need Your Money

Why do we often clash with our parents despite our love for them? Why do misunderstandings cut deeper than they should? Many of us have felt these moments when we believe we are right, yet the people we love don't see things our way.

One day, Aaraj disagreed with his father. He said something that stung:

"I don't need your money. Stop taking care of us; we will manage."

Aaraj wasn't expecting those words. They hit him like a punch to the chest.

Why would he say that? Haven't I done everything for them?

The pain turned into anger. Without another word, Aaraj stormed out of his parents' house. When Aaraj got home, the weight of the argument pressed down on him. Aaraj sat in a corner, overwhelmed.

"I am the breadwinner, Papa. Why don't you listen to me? Have I ever done anything wrong? Why don't you let me make some decisions?"

Later that night, his father called. His voice was softer. He tried to make amends, but the wound still felt raw. The next morning, Aaraj went to visit them again. Aaraj spoke briefly, kept the conversation formal, ate his favourite breakfast—*paranthas* and rajma made by his mother—and left. But the heaviness in his heart remained. He questioned Shiva and sought answers from *Him* before sleeping.

That night, Aaraj had a dream.

In the dream, his father needed to light the stove, but he couldn't find a gas lighter. Without thinking, Aaraj pulled a matchbox from his pocket and handed it to him.

In reality, his parents didn't know that Aaraj carried a matchbox with him. It was a habit—Aaraj had picked up due to smoking, something he never wanted his parents to find out.

As Aaraj was about to leave, his father handed the matchbox back to him and said,

"Take this, it's yours."

Aaraj woke up with a start. Those words echoed in his mind. "Take this, it's yours."

It was just a matchbox. Or was it?

Suddenly, Aaraj understood. His father already knew. He had seen enough of life to understand things before they were spoken. Like in the dream, he had always understood him—even when Aaraj thought he didn't.

Shiva had answered him. His pain wasn't because of his father's words but because of Aaraj's ego. He had let a moment of hurt cloud a lifetime of love. His father had never stopped understanding him—Aaraj had simply failed to see it.

That morning, Aaraj let go. The burden he had carried for days lifted, replaced by peace. Shiva's message was clear:

Some truths don't need to be spoken to be understood. Some wounds don't need to be held onto to be healed.

That dream, that sign, was his way of reminding him to surrender to let go of unnecessary pain and trust the love that had always been there.

Key Takeaway: *True wealth is not measured by money but by the values we uphold and the relationships we nurture. Our parents often seek respect, love, and emotional support more than financial assistance. Shiva teaches us that our duty is to provide and be present, listen, and honour those who shaped us.*

Chapter 41

The Call of Hanuman Ji

For several days, the thought of reading the *Hanuman Chalisa* lingered in Aaraj's mind. It felt as if Hanuman Ji, the revered Monkey God, was gently nudging him towards this sacred practice. His presence flitted through his thoughts, appearing and disappearing like a comforting shadow, as if waiting for Aaraj to acknowledge his call.

Then, one night, Aaraj had a vivid dream. In the dream, he found himself in a serene temple, kneeling before Hanuman Ji, offering flowers and praying at his feet. The atmosphere was filled with divine energy, a warmth that wrapped around his soul. When Aaraj woke up, the dream left an unshakeable conviction in his heart—He needed to pray to Hanuman Ji.

As part of his usual routine, Aaraj scrolled through Twitter that morning. Amidst the endless stream of posts, one stood out—a long thread about Tulsidas Ji, the great saint and poet who composed the *Ramcharitmanas.*

The post delved into his unwavering devotion to Hanuman Ji and the remarkable story behind the *Hanuman Chalisa.*

According to legend, Tulsidas Ji composed this sacred hymn while imprisoned in a dark dungeon at Chunar Fort, seeking Hanuman Ji's protection. Despite his confinement, his devotion remained unshaken, and in that moment of adversity, he penned a hymn that would become a beacon of strength for generations to come.

Reading this, a wave of realisation washed over Aaraj—it was as if his dream had manifested into reality through this post. The synchronicity was undeniable. Shiva had spoken to him in a way only *He* could, weaving signs into his life and leading him towards a deeper spiritual practice.

Embracing the Hanuman Chalisa

Feeling profoundly connected, Aaraj committed to incorporating the *Hanuman Chalisa* into his daily routine. Aaraj recited its verses each morning, seeking the same strength and divine protection that Tulsidas Ji found in Hanuman Ji. The more Aaraj immersed himself in the hymn, the more he felt a sense of peace and resilience settle within him.

The *Hanuman Chalisa* became his refuge. It reminded him that while life's trials are inevitable, divine grace is always within reach. Hanuman Ji's presence in his life reassured him that no challenge was too great, no burden too heavy, as long as he surrendered with faith.

Reflecting on this experience, Aaraj realises that the divine speaks to us in subtle and profound ways. Whether through dreams, scriptures, or seemingly ordinary moments, Shiva and Hanuman Ji are always guiding us, offering solace, strength, and unwavering support.

The story of Tulsidas Ji and the *Hanuman Chalisa* is a testament to this enduring truth – that faith, devotion, and divine grace can transform even the darkest moments into opportunities for spiritual growth and enlightenment.

The call of the divine is always there. All we have to do is listen.

Key Takeaway: *Divine callings come unexpectedly, urging us to trust and surrender. When Hanuman Ji calls, it reminds of faith, courage, and unwavering devotion. His presence reassures us that we are protected and guided, especially in moments of doubt and difficulty.*

Chapter 42

A Dialogue on Karma with the boss

On his way to the office one morning, Aaraj turned off the music in his car and began talking to Shiva—the eternal source of wisdom Aaraj turns to in times of doubt. Overwhelmed by frustration and the weight of unanswered questions, Aaraj asked *Him*:

"Why must a man endure so much pain when he has done nothing wrong? Why do those who live righteously—respecting life and nature—suffer undeservedly?"

Aaraj thought of those who tread lightly in this world—who conserve water and electricity even when no one is watching, avoid harming even the smallest creatures, and choose kindness in every action. Why must they suffer?

A thought crossed his mind:

Was it past-life karma? If so, was it truly fair to bear the consequences of an unknown past? Would it not be just for every soul to experience the results of their actions within the same lifetime, without the burden of carryover?

Despite his questions, Shiva remained silent. There were no whispers of guidance, no sudden clarity—just silence—a silence that felt heavy.

Aaraj reached the office, still carrying the weight of his thoughts. His boss Shalil had arrived early that day. After exchanging pleasantries, they settled into their usual discussions—routine office updates and internal matters. But as their conversation unfolded, it drifted towards something deeper.

Feeling a sense of trust, Aaraj decided to share his spiritual dilemma with him. He listened intently, his expression thoughtful. Then, with a knowing smile, he said,

"Aaraj, do you remember Arjuna's confusion on the battlefield?"

His words instantly transported him to the Kurukshetra battlefield, where Arjuna was paralysed by doubt while standing on his chariot. Facing his kin in war, he questioned the very essence of duty and righteousness. In response, Krishna, his divine guide, spoke words of profound wisdom:

"O Arjuna, this is your Karma Bhumi (land of duty), and you are here to perform your karma. You cannot escape it."

Something clicked within him. Shiva, who had been silent in the car, was now speaking through his boss. Krishna's wisdom echoed the truth Aaraj had been seeking.

No matter how unjust it seems, suffering is part of our soul's journey. Even those who live righteously face challenges, not as punishment, but as lessons that shape and refine us. We are here to live out our karma, to grow through experience, and to embrace our duty without questioning why.

It became clear that life is not about escaping suffering but about understanding it. Just as Arjuna had to fight despite his inner turmoil, we, too, must navigate our own battles with faith and acceptance.

That day, Aaraj realised something important—Shiva doesn't always answer in the way we expect. Sometimes, *He* answers through people, books, and moments of reflection. His guidance is always there, but we must be patient enough to recognise it.

Life's challenges are not roadblocks; they are stepping stones. Each struggle is an invitation to evolve, shed doubts, and surrender fully to Shiva's plan. We may not always understand why suffering exists, but faith teaches us that every experience has a purpose.

Even in silence, Shiva speaks.

Key Takeaway: *Karma is not just about rewards and punishments; it is the natural balance of cause and effect. Every action, thought, and intention shapes our destiny. True understanding of karma brings clarity, accountability, and the wisdom to act righteously without attachment to outcomes.*

Chapter 43

The Power of Communication

Aaraj is always lost in deep overthinking, constantly seeking answers to his questions. And somehow, the answers always find their way to him—through social media posts, TV shows, movies, random encounters on the road, or even unexpected conversations.

This time, the sign came from a TV series—*Suits*.

When Aaraj first started watching *Suits* on Netflix, he was instantly drawn to the character of Harvey Specter—a man of sharp intellect, unwavering confidence, and remarkable control over his emotions. His ability to communicate with clarity and authority captivated him. Harvey made decisions based on logic rather than assumptions, ensuring his actions were always guided by evidence, not emotions.

Aaraj found himself binge-watching episode after episode, eager to learn from Harvey. What fascinated him so much about Harvey was his ability to separate personal emotions from professional decisions, something Aaraj has always struggled with.

Aaraj tends to immerse his emotions in everything he does, personal or professional. When emotions take over, Aaraj fumbles, loses clarity, and sometimes even regrets his words. On the other hand, Harvey remained composed, believing that emotions, when unchecked, could be a sign of weakness. His ability to communicate effectively without letting emotions cloud his judgement was a skill Aaraj deeply admired.

One of the most powerful moments in *Suits* was when Harvey's long time secretary, Donna, decided to leave him and work for another partner, Louis Litt. She sought more emotional validation—something Harvey had always struggled to express. Despite being deeply hurt, Harvey accepted her decision and hired a new secretary.

In one particular scene, Harvey interviews candidates for the position. A long line of elegant, well-dressed women waits outside his office, all vying for the role. But instead of choosing the most conventionally attractive or impressive candidate, Harvey steps out, scans the room, and fixes his gaze on a woman who is the least expected choice—someone who doesn't fit the traditional mould. Without hesitation, he says:

"You are hired."

That moment brought tears to Aaraj's eyes. It was a powerful statement—that strength and kindness are not mutually exclusive. A man who doesn't wear his emotions on his sleeve may seem cold to the world, but in reality, he can be deeply compassionate. This scene left a lasting impact on him, reinforcing that true communication is about presence, clarity, and purpose, not just words.

As Aaraj reflected on his journey, he realised that Shiva had been guiding him towards better communication all along.

Growing up, Aaraj struggled to express himself clearly. Fear of judgement made him hesitant to speak up. He admired those who spoke fluent English, assuming language proficiency was the key to success. He often felt inferior, even when his work and dedication were recognised.

But over time, Shiva provided him with opportunities to improve. From debates in the real world to professional presentations, every experience shaped him. Slowly, Aaraj learned that language is just a tool – it is not the essence of communication.

A turning point came in 2014, when Narendra Modi became India's Prime Minister. India's transformation was evident, and the world began recognising its people's talent beyond language barriers. Social media played a crucial role, breaking down linguistic boundaries and proving that effective communication is about conveying ideas, not just speaking perfect English.

This realisation freed him from his insecurities. Aaraj no longer felt intimidated by fluent English speakers. Instead, he focused on being a better communicator, ensuring his words carried clarity, purpose, and impact, regardless of the language.

Shiva's lessons often come unexpectedly—sometimes through spiritual insights, sometimes through everyday experiences, and sometimes even through a TV series like *Suits*.

Communication is not about dominance or fluency but connection, clarity, and confidence.

Harvey Spectre taught him that strength and emotion coexist, but balance is key. Shiva reinforced that true communication is about expressing yourself authentically without letting emotions cloud your message. As Aaraj continues his journey, he strives to master the art of expression, knowing that with Shiva's guidance, he will always find his voice.

Key Takeaway: *Effective communication is not just about speaking; it's about understanding, listening, and conveying thoughts with clarity and intent. How we communicate can build relationships, resolve conflicts, and even shape our destiny. Words have power—when used wisely, they can heal, inspire, and transform lives.*

Chapter 44

The Journey to Baidhyanath Dham

One afternoon at the office, a sudden realisation struck him—Aaraj was about to start a new job, and with its demands, taking a vacation anytime soon would be nearly impossible. A thought instantly followed: This is the perfect time to visit his seventh Jyotirlinga, Baidyanath Dham, in Deoghar, Jharkhand.

Without hesitation, Aaraj called his wife Jane to seek her approval for this spontaneous spiritual journey. To his delight, she agreed immediately. Wasting no time, Aaraj searched for flight tickets and booked one without delay.

To ensure a smooth darshan, Aaraj reached out to Hari, the father of Keya (Sanya's friend), a native of Deoghar, who cautioned him about the overwhelming crowds during the Shravan month but assured him that he would connect him with someone who could help.

Aaraj left Delhi on the first Monday of Shravan month (a Pious month dedicated to Lord Shiva) and arrived in Deoghar by afternoon. Gentle rain welcomed him, adding to the mystical aura of his pilgrimage. The contact Hari provided, Alok, was incredibly kind and helpful.

Alok suggested Aaraj to get ready immediately since the temple was just a 10-minute walk from his hotel. As they approached the premises, Aaraj felt the divine energy in the air. He watched a live broadcast of the Jyotirlinga on a huge TV screen outside the sanctum and felt immensely blessed.

With the help of a pandit, Aaraj performed puja and made offerings to Bhagwan Shiva, Parvati, and other deities in the temple complex. Since the queues inside were 10 kilometres long, Aaraj poured holy water onto the Jyotirlinga through a canal outside the sanctum, bypassing the overwhelming rush.

The devotion of the pilgrims moved him – waves of devotees pushed forward, eager for a glimpse of Shiva's sacred Jyotirlinga. After the puja, the pandit advised him to return in the evening or purchase a VIP pass the next morning for a direct darshan.

Hari and Alok called back at the hotel, concerned about the massive crowds. Their words prepared him for the possibility that Aaraj might not get the darshan Aaraj longed for.

Aaraj spent the evening wandering through the streets, enjoying the local flavours, and breaking his fast with regional delicacies. By 12:30 am, exhausted but hopeful, Aaraj retired to his room.

Before sleeping, Aaraj prayed to Bhagwan Shiva, expressing his deep desire to see *Him* and asking for *His* divine help.

> *"They said that I wouldn't be able to enter the temple premises due to the rush. There's no way I'm going back to Delhi without meeting you. You brought me here, and now You alone will find a way for me to reach the temple sanctum."*

Aaraj set his alarm for 3 am, determined to wake up early and join the queue.

But destiny had other plans.

Aaraj fell into a deep sleep, unaware of time passing. Then, suddenly, a loud noise outside his hotel room startled him awake. Initially, fatigue made him ignore it.

And then, Shiva spoke to him in his sleep:

> *"You said you must have my darshan no matter what. Now, you are not ready to get up? You see what you have to do. I will not wake you up again."*

These words jolted Aaraj awake. He checked the time – 2:40 am.

Realising that Shiva himself had reminded him, Aaraj sprang out of bed, quickly bathed, dressed in fresh clothes, and rushed to the temple.

The moment Aaraj stepped out, he saw waves of people ahead and behind him, all running toward the temple. Without a second thought, Aaraj started running too and kept running.

For over a kilometre, Aaraj ran, pushing past exhaustion, guided by devotion. To his surprise, he reached the temple queue much faster than expected.

Within two hours, Aaraj stood before Bhagwan Shiva's Jyotirlinga.

At exactly 5 am, his pilgrimage was complete.

Aaraj called the pandit to cancel the VIP pass. There was no need for shortcuts when Shiva cleared his path. The pandit was pleased with Aaraj's devotion and helped him perform additional pujas, making the experience even more profound.

This journey to Baidyanath Dham was another testament to Shiva's love and presence. Despite the massive crowds, the near impossibility of a quick darshan, and his fatigue, Shiva made a way for him.

This experience reinforced his faith—when your devotion is pure, Shiva answers in ways beyond logic.

With a heart full of gratitude, Aaraj left Deoghar, knowing that this sacred visit had deepened his connection with Shiva and brought him one step closer to him.

––––––––––

Key Takeaway: *A pilgrimage is not just a physical journey but a spiritual awakening. The path to a sacred place like Baidyanath Dham is filled with tests of faith, endurance, and self-discovery. True devotion lies in surrendering to the divine, trusting the journey, and embracing the lessons along the way.*

Chapter 45

From Design to Product

Aaraj had reached the pinnacle of his career in Design, holding the top position in his company *(Hindustan Times)*. But instead of feeling accomplished, Aaraj felt disheartened.

Design is often undervalued in India—placed after Sales, Tech, Product and Marketing. In contrast, Western companies embrace Design Thinking, focusing on creating better user experiences through thoughtful design. But here, the emphasis is almost always on cost, revenue, and profits. Companies become so fixated on achieving targets and completing KRAs that they overlook a simple truth:

If users are happy, the money will follow.

Despite his success, Aaraj felt a deep dissatisfaction. He would often ask Shiva:

"Why is this not working? I need to do more – I can reach much higher. This design job is not giving me the value I seek."

During these moments of introspection, Aaraj discovered a new passion—Product Management.

While working in Design, Aaraj had already created numerous digital products, but his superiors often overlooked his contributions. He knew he could do more. Aaraj wanted to break the perception that only those from Tech backgrounds could excel in Product roles, but Design people could excel too.

Aaraj strongly believed that a foundation in Design was just as valuable, if not more, for crafting successful products.

With this newfound conviction, Aaraj started searching for Head of Product roles, even though his official title was still Head of Design.

This transition was far from easy.

For nearly two years of searching, while working at his last job, Aaraj actively pursued a shift into Product Management.

Aaraj often pleaded with Shiva, asking:

"Why can't I find a Product role when I know I can excel in it?"

No matter how much effort Aaraj put in, nothing seemed to work. The wait was long, the uncertainty exhausting. But Shiva had a plan all along.

After 2 years of searching and praying, Aaraj finally landed a Director of Product Management role.

His new company specialises in Print Automation and Digital News Publication, a field in which Aaraj has spent his entire career. When Aaraj realised this, an overwhelming sense of happiness and gratitude filled his heart.

This was not just a new job. It was the perfect match for his experience, expertise, and passion.

What made this transition even more special was the uniqueness of his role—it was newly created, tailored to his distinct skill set.

The company was filled with Tech experts and engineers, but here was Aaraj—the only non-Tech professional yet perfectly positioned for this role.

It was as if Shiva had carved out this opportunity just for him, preparing him throughout his career for this very moment.

This experience deepened his faith manifold.

Looking back, Aaraj now understands:

→ Shiva never denied his wish—*He* was preparing him for the perfect role.

→ His frustrations, struggles, and long wait were all part of the journey leading him to something far greater than Aaraj had imagined.

→ When the time is right, the universe aligns everything perfectly.

Aaraj was humbled and grateful beyond words.

This journey has been a profound lesson—when held with faith and patience, our deepest desires send messages to the divine.

And when the moment is right, Shiva ensures everything falls into place.

Aaraj feels incredibly fortunate to have Shiva by his side, guiding him through life's challenges and triumphs.

This chapter of Aaraj's life has taught us:

→ Success is not just about reaching the top – it's about finding purpose and fulfilment in the journey.

→ We are never alone; divine support is always with us.

→ With faith, patience, and the right mindset, we can achieve even our deepest desires.

Yet again, Shiva has shown him that He is always listening, guiding, and preparing the best for him.

Key Takeaway: *Every idea starts as a vision, but its potential is realised through execution. The journey from Design to Product requires perseverance, adaptability, and faith. Just like in life, bringing something to fruition demands creative energy and strategic action, guided by a higher purpose.*

Chapter 46

Lessons from Power, Humility, and Karma

On a day when no one remained untouched by the influence of political agendas, June 4, 2024, stood as a significant moment for India—the day election results were to be announced. Like everyone else, Aaraj, too, was caught in a whirlwind of confusion over the final outcome. His mind was restless, filled with questions, and he turned to Bhagwan Shiva, seeking clarity and understanding.

Who will win? Will the BJP get a full majority, lose, or form a coalition government?

The exit polls from major media houses had confidently predicted a sweeping victory for the ruling party, BJP. Everywhere Aaraj turned, people were certain that a two-thirds majority was inevitable.

Yet, amidst this widespread optimism, Aaraj felt uncertain.

A part of him wanted to believe in the predictions, but a lingering doubt remained. Something inside told him to stay cautious, not to celebrate (a staunch BJP supporter) before the results were truly in, though Aaraj wanted those predictions to come true.

When the results were finally declared, his doubts were confirmed.

Yes, the BJP had formed the government, but not with the overwhelming majority that had been anticipated. They now required the support of allies to secure power.

He was perplexed.

Over the years, he had observed the government's sincere efforts to work for the people, especially in contrast to the corruption of previous administrations. So, Aaraj turned to Shiva, seeking an answer.

The response Aaraj received was profound:

Power, if not handled with humility, can lead to a downfall.

The election outcome was not as favourable for the BJP as expected. They fell short of their projected number of seats, yet still managed to form the government. But what went wrong despite the strong wave of support in their favour? Was it overconfidence, shifting public sentiment, or an unexpected undercurrent of opposition? The results left many, including Aaraj, pondering the deeper forces at play behind the numbers.

Even the most well-intentioned leaders can falter if they allow power to cloud their judgement. This was a lesson not just for him but also for Prime Minister Narendra Modi.

He was reminded that leading a nation is not a solo endeavour—it requires:

→ Collaboration

→ Humility

→ Recognition of every team member's contributions

This election outcome was not a defeat but a divine lesson, reinforcing that no leader succeeds alone. Governance, like life, is a team game.

Another moment of reflection came during the Paris Olympics.

Binny (name changed), an Indian wrestler, was on the brink of winning a gold medal for India. Her journey had been one of perseverance and determination, overcoming immense adversity.

But then, the unexpected happened—

Just before her final match, she was disqualified due to issues with her weight category. This cost her the final bout and took away her previously won medal.

The day before her disqualification, Aaraj had been filled with questions.

This was the same athlete who had previously protested against the government (BJP), allegedly influenced by opposition forces or blinded by the temptation of power.

Aaraj wondered:

→ What if she won the gold?

→ Would she receive a congratulatory call from Narendra Modi, Prime Minister of India, like other medallists?

→ Would it spark another political controversy?

Aaraj couldn't shake off the unease.

But the next morning, the narrative shifted entirely.

Binny didn't win – in fact, she didn't even compete in the final match.

Her disqualification became a powerful lesson in humility and the workings of karma.

This moment reaffirmed a fundamental truth:

No matter how much effort we put in, we cannot afford to be complacent.

Our actions have consequences, and if we stray from the path of righteousness, our past deeds will catch up with us in ways we least expect.

Through these experiences, Shiva continues to teach us:

→ Power must be wielded with humility.

→ Success without gratitude can be fleeting.

→ Karma always finds its way.

As much as we strive for personal victories, we must remain grounded, aware, and righteous in our pursuits.

Shiva's subtle guidance in these moments has shown him that the answers we seek often go beyond our personal desires. They touch upon the collective wisdom that governs the universe.

This journey has taught him that true fulfilment doesn't come from personal success alone.

It comes from:

→ Understanding life's deeper lessons

→ Recognising the importance of humility in the face of power

→ Staying committed to righteousness, no matter the challenges

Aaraj continues to walk this path, knowing that Shiva is always there, offering wisdom—not just for him, but for the world.

———

Key Takeaway: *True power is not in dominance but in humility. The balance of power and humility defines one's karma—how we use our influence determines our spiritual and worldly outcomes. When we align our actions with righteousness, karma ensures justice, sooner or later.*

Chapter 47

Navigating Loss, Seeking Answers, and Finding Guidance

August 18th, 2024—the day Aaraj's world changed forever.

His father passed away, leaving him devastated.

Aaraj had fulfilled all the rituals and last rites, including his cremation on the last Monday of Shravan (yet another plan of Shiva), yet the pain remained raw.

Aaraj kept asking Shiva,

"Why? Why did this happen so suddenly?"

His father had been healthy, fit, and active. He practised yoga every morning and took evening walks daily. There were no warning signs, no indication that anything was wrong.

But then, in an instant, everything changed.

That evening, his father came home and told his mother,

"My left arm is in severe pain… and I can't stop sweating."

Within minutes, the pain became unbearable. His mother, panicked, called Aaraj.

Aaraj rushed to the home in fifteen minutes, but by then his condition had deteriorated rapidly. He was having a major heart attack.

They took him to the hospital.

Despite their best efforts, despite the doctors' intervention, he passed away the next day.

It all happened in the blink of an eye.

One day, he was healthy and full of life, and the next, he was gone.

Even months after his passing, Aaraj was still searching for answers.

Aaraj asked Shiva every day, but he hadn't received any yet.

He knew that the answers would come in time, and when they did, *he* would share them. But the hardest part was knowing how unexpected it all was.

Just a few days before his father's passing, Aaraj had stood on the terrace, praying to Shiva.

"Bless me so I can give my parents the life they deserve – comfort, luxury, everything they sacrificed for me."

And then, just like that, he was gone.

The suddenness of it all felt like a cruel twist of fate.

As if his personal grief wasn't heavy enough, his professional life was also at a crossroads.

Aaraj had joined a new company, Director of Product and Management, just two weeks before his father's passing. He took three weeks of bereavement leave, but even when he returned, he struggled to find his footing.

This new role was completely different from what Aaraj had done before.

Aaraj was no longer focused on design. Instead, he navigated internal office politics issues and tried to adapt while still processing his loss.

Every day, doubts weighed him down.

Was I ready for this? Could I handle it all?

The grief of losing his father and the pressure of settling into a new role made everything feel heavier.

In these moments of doubt, Aaraj kept turning to Shiva, asking him for clarity.

One night, lost in thought, Aaraj had a dream.

Aaraj saw Shiva's abode nestled among the clouds, with golden architecture against a vast blue sky.

It was serene, divine, and peaceful.

For a moment, Aaraj felt a deep sense of calm.

But then, Aaraj got distracted.

Instead of absorbing the vision, Aaraj started scrolling through his phone.

And just like that, when Aaraj looked up again, the vision was gone.

The next day, work was exhausting.

That evening, feeling drained, Aaraj went back to the terrace for a walk.

Aaraj asked Shiva again for guidance.

And in that moment, it felt like he was gently reminding him—

"Stop wasting your time on distractions."

Aaraj realised scrolling mindlessly wasn't helping him.

Aaraj needed to focus on something meaningful.

That's when Aaraj decided to turn to reading.

Aaraj opened Flipboard, his favourite app, and started exploring topics that genuinely interested him.

While browsing, Aaraj stumbled upon a course that could help him in his present job—something He had been curious about.

On impulse, Aaraj signed up.

Little did Aaraj know that this course would change everything.

It helped him create a Product roadmap for his company—something Aaraj had been struggling with.

As he worked through the course, Aaraj realised:

None of this would have happened if Shiva hadn't nudged him in this direction through his dream.

He guided him away from distractions and towards something that would help him grow professionally and personally.

Shiva was always there through all his doubts, grief, and struggles.

Even when Aaraj couldn't see the bigger picture, he worked in the background, guiding and showing him the way.

His presence *gives him strength, clarity and faith in the journey ahead.*

And for that, Aaraj is eternally grateful.

Key Takeaway: Loss shakes the foundation of our existence, but in seeking answers, we open ourselves to divine guidance. Shiva's presence is felt in the signs, dreams, and experiences that shape our path, reminding us that even in grief, we are never alone. Move on as life keeps moving on.

Chapter 48

The Road to Patience

*S*hiva's guidance doesn't always arrive in grand moments *— it often* comes through life's simplest routines, like driving to the office.

Lately, *his* inner voice had urged him to practice patience on the road. "Avoid honking. Let go of frustration. Drive calmly," *he* seemed to whisper every time Aaraj gripped the steering wheel.

But patience doesn't come easily to him, especially when Aaraj sees reckless drivers making careless mistakes. Yet, Shiva's message was clear:

If I didn't control my impatience, I could damage my car, something I was planning to sell soon and buy a new one.

Aaraj heard *his* warning. But one day, he chose not to listen.

That morning, Aaraj drove with frustration. He honked, rushed, and reacted. And then, it happened—a rickshaw driver scraped his car, shattering the side mirror.

It was a sharp blow to Aaraj's pride, though it was not costly. He got it repaired and promised himself to be more mindful.

But just days later, another incident occurred – a mini-truck brushed against his car. Anger surged within him.

Aaraj clenched his fists and muttered,

"Shiva, if you are teaching me patience, then please give me a sign. Yes, I heard the loud scraping noise, I know. But if this is a lesson in patience, please don't damage the car too much. I will understand your sign."

Aaraj asked for proof—something to confirm that he was meant to learn from this experience. When he checked his car, he saw that despite the loud scrape, there was no significant damage. That was his sign. A lesson in restraint and a reminder to trust *His* guidance.

The Same Lesson, A Different Setting

Patience wasn't just a lesson for the road—it was also a test Aaraj faced in his new job. Eager to prove himself, Aaraj jumped into everything, asked too many questions, and tried to do more than his role required.

In his mind, he was being proactive. But to others, it looked like impatience.

Soon, Aaraj was called into a meeting. The message was clear: "Slow down. Focus on your primary responsibilities."

Aaraj felt a twinge of disappointment. Had he rushed into things again? But as he reflected, he realised Shiva was teaching him the same lesson—whether behind the wheel or in his career, impatience had its consequences.

During this phase of self-reflection, Aaraj stumbled upon a podcast by Osho—another sign from Shiva, delivered through an unexpected source.

Osho (Indian godman and philosopher) spoke about anger as an energy that, if left uncontrolled, takes over our actions. When we lose our temper, we surrender control to the very person we're angry at.

His words struck him. Impatience is just another form of anger. And anger, if misdirected, only harms us. Osho shared a fable that resonated deeply with Aaraj:

A rabbit once challenged a fox, questioning its authenticity. The fox, unsure of itself, sought validation from a lion. But the lion's wisdom was simple: True confidence doesn't come from outside approval – it comes from within.

That was the final lesson Aaraj needed. He had been seeking validation from other drivers, from his colleagues, from life itself. But just like the fox, Aaraj didn't need external confirmation. If Aaraj was doing the right thing, he had to trust in his own judgement.

This phase of his journey taught him profound truths:

→ Patience isn't just about waiting—it's about trusting the process.

→ Anger and frustration are energies that can be channelled into growth.

→ Confidence doesn't come from others—it comes from within.

Even now, when impatience creeps in, Aaraj reminds himself that Shiva is always guiding him. Whether through a broken mirror, a scraped car, or a podcast, Aaraj randomly stumbles upon—*His* messages are everywhere.

As Aaraj learns to listen, he finds himself becoming calmer, stronger, and more centred with each passing day.

Key Takeaway: *Patience is not just about waiting; it's about maintaining faith and inner peace while waiting. Shiva teaches that true strength lies in surrendering to divine timing, trusting that everything unfolds as it should.*

Chapter 49

The Dark Fantasies Warning

Last night, Aaraj had a dream that left him unsettled. Aaraj found himself sleeping alongside his wife in a place they weren't supposed to be—something felt off, almost illegitimate. The scene shifted, and suddenly, Aaraj was struggling with police officers, unable to free himself from their grip. No matter how hard Aaraj tried to negotiate or reason with them, he remained trapped in their hold.

Aaraj woke up abruptly, his mind racing. Was this just a random dream, or was there a deeper message hidden within? Aaraj tried to recall his thoughts before drifting off to sleep, searching for a connection between his subconscious and the divine. Then it struck him—this wasn't just a dream. It was a warning.

Shiva had sent him a sign, a clear cautionary message about the consequences of seeking fleeting pleasures, even in ways that seemed harmless on the surface. The dream wasn't just about getting caught; it was about restraint, about the price of indulgence, and the unseen repercussions of giving in to desires.

Desires, when suppressed for too long, often manifest as frustration, anger, or reckless mistakes when finally unleashed. For him, it had been a few months without intimacy. Though masturbation had provided temporary relief, the prolonged abstinence had begun stirring deep-seated fantasies within him. The urge to break free, to indulge, to seek a momentary escape, had grown stronger.

Aaraj had been contemplating a night out with his friend Neeraj—a carefree evening of partying, flirting, and indulgence, something akin to a bachelor's escapade. But after this dream, Aaraj couldn't ignore the sign. It was a clear indication that even a seemingly harmless plan could lead to unwanted consequences. Shiva had stepped in, whispering through the symbols in his dream, urging him to reconsider his actions.

And so, Aaraj did. He dropped the plan (making with Neeraj) without a second thought. The momentary thrill wasn't worth the potential fallout. The guilt and suppressed urges that had been clouding his mind suddenly eased. A wave of relief washed over him, as if Shiva himself had reassured him—Aaraj had made the right choice.

This experience reaffirmed his faith in Shiva's guidance. Even in his weakest moments, even when his mind wandered towards temptations, *He* was there, steering him away from mistakes that could cost him his peace. It was yet another reminder that true liberation comes not from fulfilling desires recklessly but from understanding when to exercise restraint.

That night, in his darkest fantasies, Shiva's light shone the brightest, showing him the way forward.

Key Takeaway: If left unchecked, temptations and desires can lead to consequences that disrupt inner peace. Shiva's guidance through dreams and signs helps us make the right choices, reminding us that self-discipline and awareness are key to avoiding regret.

Chapter 50

Song Conversations with the Divine

Each day begins with an invocation to his beloved Baba—his presence fills him with purpose and courage, guiding him through life's unpredictable journey.

When emotions weigh you down, you seek *His* presence everywhere, always searching for answers. In moments of despair, some find comfort in old, soulful songs that touch their hearts. But for Aaraj, solace came through Shiva's songs—where he felt truly immersed in devotion. Songs like *"Shiv samah rahe mujh mein aur main shoonya ho raha hoon"*, *"Bhole Baba Ji, jholi bhar do"*, *"Mere Bheeter Bhole Tu Bole"* and more such Shiva songs became his refuge, drawing him closer to the divine.

The verses of these songs echoed within him, capturing the essence of his sacred connection with Shiva. Aaraj often found hidden meanings and messages in the lyrics—signs from Shiva guiding him on his journey.

In moments of joy, Aaraj laughs freely, embracing the warmth of his love. But in sorrow, He weeps in quiet solitude, knowing He sees every tear and every unspoken pain. *His* presence, though unseen, is as real as the air Aaraj breathes, wrapping around him like a gentle embrace.

In these verses, Aaraj found true peace, as if every song carried the answers he was seeking. Life's challenges stood before him like towering giants, but with Baba's wisdom and strength, he remained steadfast. He no longer needed the world's validation to define his worth, for Baba had filled him with an unshakeable inner strength.

In a world rife with deception and selfishness, his purity stands as a beacon of truth. *He* sees through the masks of pretenders, discerning the sincerity of his heart with unerring clarity. With Shiva by his side, Aaraj confronts his fears, sheds his insecurities, and walks forward with fearless conviction.

When despair grips his soul, Baba breathes new life into his weary spirit. His boundless love and compassion become his shield against hopelessness, his torch in the darkest of times. No setback is permanent, no sorrow unconquerable—for he is with him, whispering words of wisdom in the silent spaces of his heart.

In a world that often seeks to undermine your confidence and break your spirit, Baba remains your unwavering ally. Trust in his divine plan, for *He* resides within you, guiding you, empowering you, and reminding you that you were never meant to walk this path alone. With faith in Baba, you will always rise stronger, wiser, and victorious.

Key Takeaway: Divine messages can come in unexpected forms, including music and lyrics. When we are attuned to the signs around us, even a simple song can become a medium for spiritual connection, guidance, and reassurance from the divine.

Chapter 51

ShivGans: Recognising Shiva's Avatars in Everyday Life

Bhagwan Shiva does not always reveal himself in his true form. Instead, *he* manifests through avatars—subtle yet powerful presences that guide, warn, reward, and sometimes even discipline us. These avatars often appear in the most unexpected ways, working through ordinary people who unknowingly serve as vessels of divine intervention.

As a frequent traveller, Aaraj has encountered this phenomenon firsthand, not in grand temples or sacred spaces, but in the humblest of places—roadside dhabas, small tea stalls, and modest hotels. In these seemingly ordinary encounters, Aaraj has felt an unspoken connection with strangers, sensing the presence of Shiva's devotees and experiencing moments of mutual assistance and understanding. It feels as if Shiva himself orchestrates these meetings, ensuring that they help and support one another at just the right time.

Aaraj experiences them every now and then. One such experience stands out vividly. During a long journey, Aaraj stopped at a small roadside dhaba for a quick meal. The owner, a kind and unassuming man, welcomed him warmly. As they spoke, Aaraj felt an inexplicable sense of familiarity—something deeper than mere hospitality. As their conversation unfolded, he shared his struggles, aspirations, and deep faith in Shiva. Moved by his sincerity, Aaraj found himself offering words of encouragement, unknowingly serving as a conduit for Shiva's guidance.

Reflecting on this, Aaraj is reminded of a scene from the movie "OMG 2", where Shiva sends his devoted follower (played by Akshay Kumar – Bollywood actor) to assist another follower (played by Pankaj Tripathi – Bollywood actor). The guidance is not direct – it comes in subtle hints, nudges, and the wisdom of an ordinary man who carries the essence of Shiva within him. Similarly, in his own experiences, Aaraj has met individuals whose words and actions mirror Shiva's divine wisdom and compassion, guiding him just when he needed it most.

However, these encounters are not limited to chance meetings with strangers. During a business trip, Aaraj stayed at a modest hotel, where he struck up a conversation with the receptionist. As they exchanged stories and beliefs, Aaraj discovered he was a devout follower of Shiva. Despite coming from different backgrounds, they connected instantly, as if they were kindred spirits on a shared spiritual path. In that moment, Aaraj realised something profound—Shiva's presence transcends all barriers. *He* is not bound by language, culture, or location; *His* energy flows through those who carry faith in their hearts.

These experiences serve as powerful reminders that Shiva's avatars are not confined to ancient scriptures or mythology. They are alive and active in the world around us, in the people we meet, and in the wisdom they share. Shiva reveals himself not through grand miracles but through the simplest gestures – a kind word from a stranger, a timely piece of advice, or an unexpected helping hand in a time of need.

Key Takeaway: Shiva manifests in countless ways around us—through people, events, and even challenges. Recognising these divine avatars in our daily lives helps us stay connected to his guidance, reinforcing that we are never alone on our journey.

Chapter 52

The Stock Market of Life

Aaraj had been investing in mutual funds for years, but with limited knowledge of stock performance, he struggled to understand why some funds performed better than others. He often wondered how asset managers controlled or infused additional capital into these funds.

In his quest for understanding, Aaraj drew a unique analogy—comparing the stock market and asset managers to Shiva and His followers. Just as people often say, *"He is lucky"* when someone seems to receive more than they deserve, Aaraj saw a deeper connection. He realised that just as an asset manager strategically allocates resources for growth, Shiva, too, bestows wisdom, opportunities, and guidance based on one's karmic balance. Through this analogy, Aaraj sought to bridge the complexities of the stock market with the workings of divine intervention, making it more relatable to everyday life.

Life operates much like the stock market—a dynamic and ever-changing ecosystem where each individual represents a stock, with its own unique potential, challenges, and growth trajectories. But unlike human investors who speculate, Bhagwan Shiva is the ultimate investor, divinely orchestrating the allocation of resources and blessings based on the performance of these "stocks."

Imagine for a moment that Shiva is the Asset Manager, overseeing the grand marketplace of human existence. *His* investment strategy is not driven by mere profit but by spiritual growth, karma, and contribution to the greater good.

Let's explore this theory through a few scenarios.

Consider Individuals Poorvi and Vinni, both navigating the unpredictable waves of life. Poorvi is struggling, caught in a cycle of self-doubt, negativity, and inaction. Meanwhile, Vinni is thriving—not just for personal success, but by uplifting those around them. From Shiva's perspective, Poorvi represents a low-performing stock, stagnant and in need of transformation, while Vinni is a high-performing stock, actively adding value to the universe.

What does Shiva do? *He* directs more resources, energy, and divine support towards Vinni, allowing them to grow further. Poorvi, on the other hand, does not receive the same level of immediate intervention until Poorvi makes an effort to change.

Now, shift the focus to a community coming together to help a struggling member. As people unite in compassion, their collective "stock" rises, catching Shiva's attention. Recognising their commitment to selflessness, Shiva intervenes, infusing them with his grace, empowering them to continue their work and strengthening their bond.

However, Shiva is not just an observer of human behaviour—he is also a strategic investor. *He* recognises that some souls, though struggling, have immense untapped potential. Just as a seasoned investor might inject capital into an undervalued stock, Shiva extends his guidance to those who seek it, nudging them towards their highest self, as with Aaraj.

This analogy offers a profound truth:

> *Our actions determine the divine investment we receive. By engaging in acts of kindness, integrity, and self-improvement, we naturally attract Shiva's grace, just as a well-managed stock attracts positive returns.*

Shiva does not play favourites. *He* invests in each one of us equally, offering his grace without bias or discrimination. But just like any investment, the returns *He* receives depend on what we give back—our compassion, integrity, and kindness.

People often say,

"That person is lucky; they have Shiva's blessings."

But what they fail to see is *why* that person is lucky. They are receiving more because they are giving more. The more you radiate kindness, uplift others, and walk in truth, the more Shiva entrusts you with his divine abundance.

His blessings are not random – they are reflections of our own actions. If you truly seek his presence, be his instrument. Share love, help those in need, and live with honesty. The more you give, the more he gives back. This is the divine law of investment.

———

Key Takeaway: Life, like the stock market, is unpredictable and filled with highs and lows. Patience, resilience, and trust in divine timing are key to navigating uncertainties. In investing, wise decisions and faith in the long-term process lead to growth and fulfilment.

Chapter 53

Whatever Happens, Happens for Good

Aaraj's life is a journey of unpredictable twists, unexpected setbacks, and moments of triumph. Yet, behind every challenge lies a lesson, and within every hardship, there is a hidden blessing. Through faith in Bhagwan Shiva, we begin to see that everything happens for a reason, guiding us towards self-discovery and spiritual awakening.

It is easy to feel overwhelmed when things don't go as planned. Frustration, despair, and doubt creep in, making us question why we must endure pain and struggle. But Shiva's presence shines brightest in our darkest moments, offering us solace, strength, and the assurance that we are never truly alone.

Through the wisdom passed down by our ancestors, we learn that every difficulty is a divine invitation to grow. It is not merely the events that shape us but how we respond to them. Shiva does not simply remove obstacles; instead, *He* grants us the vision to see them as stepping stones, preparing us for something greater.

Often, we fail to recognise the hidden grace within life's hardships. A closed door may be saving us from unforeseen harm. A delay may be aligning us with the perfect opportunity. A painful experience may be shaping us into a stronger, wiser version of ourselves. When we surrender to Shiva's guidance, we begin to trust the journey—even when we don't fully understand it.

There are countless moments when Shiva shields us without us even realising it. *He* redirects our path, subtly steering us away from unseen dangers. *His* guidance is everywhere—in the whisper of intuition, in the gentle nudges of fate, and in the serendipitous events that shape our lives. If we learn to listen, we can begin to see his divine hand at work.

Walking the path of faith means embracing the truth that every setback is a preparation for a comeback, and every trial is an opportunity to rise stronger than before. Faith does not mean a life without struggles—it means knowing that no struggle is ever in vain.

In the end, it is not challenges but our response to them that defines us. It is not our fears that shape our destiny but our faith in Bhagwan Shiva's guiding presence.

→ For when we trust in *Him*, we find clarity.

→ When we surrender to him, we find peace.

→ And when we walk with *Him*, we find our way home.

Key Takeaway: *Even in moments of struggle and disappointment, there is a hidden divine plan at work. What seems like a setback today may be a necessary step towards something better. Trusting Shiva's wisdom allows us to embrace life's unfolding journey with faith and acceptance.*

Chapter 54

The Weight of Loss and Detachment

It has been six months since Aaraj's father passed away in August 2024, yet the emptiness lingers. His presence had always been a source of inspiration, pushing him to grow, to do better. But now, with him gone, Aaraj feels unmoored. The drive to achieve, to strive for more, has faded. Any disturbance to his peace, Aaraj simply shrugs off. Nothing seems to matter the way it once did.

One question haunted him last night, keeping him from sleep—

What if his mother, his sole responsibility now, apart from his daughter and wife, also leaves him for her heavenly abode? How will Aaraj survive without her? The thought was unbearable.

A single answer emerged from the depths of his mind:

I will leave everything behind. I imagined myself going to the hills, dedicating my life to sadhana, abandoning this material world. I would hand over my assets, sever all ties, and walk away forever.

But then another question arose – "How will I survive?"

The answer came quickly— "I will survive like other saints and sages."

And if I receive nothing? I will plant a sign, just as people do in America, stating my reason to seek help (beg). Someone will help. And if that fails? Would I return to the chaos of the city? Could I handle it?

These unsettling thoughts consumed Aaraj until he finally got up to freshen up, seeking a distraction.

Half-awake, Aaraj scrolled through Twitter. And then, as if Shiva himself had answered (like always) his doubts, he came across a post:

"Eternity only chooses the brave ones who can battle."

Aaraj smiled. Shiva was speaking to him. *He* was telling him that Aaraj would embark on his chosen path only when he was truly ready. Until then, he must not be consumed by worry. He must surrender his fears to him. The realisation gave him instant relief.

As Aaraj returned from dropping his daughter at the bus stop, another fear surfaced—this time about his livelihood. Aaraj had quit his job, prioritising his mental peace over ambition.

But what if the future turned unfavourable? What if I struggled financially?

Once again, Shiva guided him to an answer. As Aaraj scrolled, another post appeared:

"Whether situations are favourable or not, warriors never leave the ground."
(Accompanied by an image of Shri Krishna and Arjuna on the battlefield.)

It was as if Shiva whispered in his ear:

"Keep doing what you are doing. Do not leave the ground. Let go of your fears—I am with you."

This moment reminded him of an eternal truth—faith is not the absence of fear, but the courage to walk forward despite it. When faced with loss, detachment, or uncertainty, surrendering to a higher power does not mean giving up; it means trusting the path that is unfolding.

His doubts still surface, but Shiva always answers. *He* rescues him from his turmoil, time and again. And as long as *He* walks with him, Aaraj will not be lost.

***Key Takeaway:** Loss tests our strength, and detachment teaches us resilience. While grief can feel overwhelming, true surrender to Shiva helps us find peace in impermanence, guiding us to move forward without being consumed by sorrow.*

Chapter 55

Choosing Peace Over Everything Else

Life has always been a series of challenges—some expected, some unforeseen. But one truth has remained constant: change.

Change has shaped Aaraj's journey, tested his patience, and forced him to re-evaluate his priorities.

And now, standing at yet another crossroads, Aaraj realises there is only one thing he truly seeks—peace.

He left his job.

Not out of impulse, not out of frustration, but out of a conscious decision—one that had been growing inside him for a long time.

The corporate world—with its endless targets, hierarchies, and the relentless race for recognition—had never been his true calling.

For years, Aaraj fought to prove his worth, to make an impact, to climb higher, and to defend actual users.

Yet, no matter how far Aaraj went, something always felt missing.

After his father's passing, Aaraj immersed himself in work, hoping it would help him move forward.

But instead of healing, he found himself drowning.

The weight of grief and professional expectations became overwhelming.

There was no joy, no fulfilment—only the constant pressure to perform or succumb to the pressure of office politics.

Aaraj turned to Shiva and asked,

"Why do I feel this way? Shouldn't I be grateful for my achievements? Why do I feel so… empty?"

And then the answer became clear—Because the soul was not at peace.

→ Aaraj had no backup plan.

→ Aaraj had no job lined up.

But he had faith—faith that Shiva would lead the way.

For the first time, Aaraj wasn't making decisions based on society's expectations or financial security.

Aaraj was deciding purely for his well-being and thinking solely about attaining one goal - Peace.

There are moments of doubt when Aaraj wonders if he has made the right choice.

But every time Aaraj seeks reassurance, Shiva sends him a sign.

He reminds Aaraj—

The world is full of distractions. His purpose is not to chase what society deems as success, but to walk the path that brings him peace.

The world may not understand this choice.

Some may call it reckless.

Others may call it brave.

But for him, it is neither.

It is simply necessary.

Aaraj no longer seeks validation from others.

His path is his alone, and he trusts that Shiva will illuminate the way.

A New Chapter Begins

This is not the end of his journey.

It is just the beginning of a new one—

One that Aaraj will walk with unwavering faith, embracing whatever comes next.

And when Aaraj looks back, he knows that he will never regret choosing peace over everything else.

The story continues – and Aaraj is ready.

Key Takeaway: *True fulfilment comes not from external achievements but from inner peace. When faced with turmoil, choosing tranquillity over chaos allows us to align with Shiva's will and navigate life with clarity and purpose.*

Afterward

We are shaped by what we see, hear, consume, and experience each day. Our thoughts, beliefs, and perceptions reflect our daily intake, forming the lens through which we view the world. As Aaraj looks back on his journey, he realises how deeply these influences have shaped his faith, convictions, and spiritual path.

Through life's trials and tribulations, Shiva emerged as his anchor, guiding force, and source of strength. Every challenge became a lesson, every struggle a stepping stone towards deeper faith. This book is a reflection of that journey—one that began with questions but led to divine answers woven into the fabric of daily life.

For you, Shiva may take a different form. You may see *Him* as Ram, Krishna, Hanuman, Devi Maa, Guru Nanak, Jesus, or any divine force that resonates with your soul. What truly matters is your belief—the unwavering conviction that the divine resides within, always guiding and protecting.

This book is not just a collection of Aaraj's experiences—it is a testament to faith, a reminder that belief has the power to transform lives. If there is one message Aaraj hopes to leave behind, it is this:

With unshakeable faith in the divine, anything is possible.

No matter how uncertain life seems, faith is the anchor that keeps us steady. Shiva is always with us, leading the way, whispering answers in ways we least expect. We only need to open our hearts to recognise them.

May our journeys be filled with wisdom, strength, and Shiva's boundless grace. May we walk forward with faith in our hearts, knowing that every path leads us closer to the ultimate truth.

Thank you for walking Aaraj's journey through these pages. May Shiva's grace illuminate your path, just as it has illuminated Aaraj's.

---

*Note: *This book is not intended to defame or hurt anyone mentioned within its pages. The name references are included to illustrate how Shiva's wisdom transcends all boundaries, delivering blessings to some and lessons to others.*

www.ingramcontent.com/pod-product-compliance
Lightning Source LLC
Chambersburg PA
CBHW051154130726
47988CB00005B/2126